M
AND OTHERS

MORTALS AND OTHERS

American Essays 1931 - 1935

Bertrand Russell

Edited by Harry Ruja
with a new introduction by John G. Slater

London and New York

First published George Allen & Unwin 1975

Reprinted with new introduction 1996
by Routledge
11 New Fetter Lane, London EC4P 4EE

Simultaneously published in the USA and Canada
by Routledge
29 West 35th Street, New York, NY 10001

Routledge is an International Thomson Publishing Company

Typeset in Baskerville
Printed and bound in Great Britain by
Mackays of Chatham PLC, Chatham, Kent

British Library Cataloguing in Publication Data
A catalogue record for this book is available from the British Library

Library of Congress Cataloguing in Publication Data
A catalogue record for this book has been requested

ISBN 0–415–12585–5

'Every man would be God, if it were possible; some few find it difficult to admit the impossibility'.

Bertrand Russell

INTRODUCTION

Bertrand Russell's occasional essays typically exhibit both the serious and the less serious side of his personality. Even if the subject of an essay is light and even, perhaps, frivolous-sounding, he still manages to come up with an angle on it which is worthy of serious consideration. Consider, for instance, 'Who May Use Lipstick?'. In his answer to this question he notes that the largest group of women who may *not* use it are school teachers, which leads him to consider the reasons behind this particular prohibition, and, consequently, to the sexual constraints under which these women work, and, finally, to the effect these constraints are likely to have on the children under their tutelage. No one will doubt that he has reached important matters here, although hardly anyone would have expected it when they read the title. The ability to surprise his readers is one of Russell's enduring characteristics.

The essays in this volume vary considerably in their structure, for Russell was inclined to let the content determine the overall logic of his treatment of it. There are, however, recurring features which mark them as his, unmistakably. Among them are his use of historical (or contemporary) events to illustrate a point, of appeals to his own experience to sharpen the force of what he wants to say, of wit to trap the hostile reader into giving a point otherwise dismissed out of hand sympathetic attention, of logical analysis to lay out the alternatives requiring discussion, and of a dazzling command of the English language which never fails to charm his readers.

After philosophy Russell was probably most interested in

history, especially when it came to his recreational reading. During the course of a very long life he wrote a number of essays designed to encourage others to share this passion; one of them, 'The Consolations of History', is reprinted here. In his opinion a knowledge of history is essential to being civilised; he would certainly have agreed with his fellow philosopher, George Santayana, that 'those who cannot remember the past are condemned to repeat it.' History lays out for us the ideas that have been tried and found to work, as well as those that have been tried and found not to work; consequently, those particular dead ends can, if knowledge of them becomes widely disseminated, be avoided in future. From the study of history we also learn something very important about the range of actual human behaviour, such knowledge tends to make us more tolerant of those with whom time obliges us to live. Take, for instance, this marvellous illustration of collective human gullibility from 'An Outline of Intellectual Rubbish' in Russell's *Unpopular Essays* (p. 145):

> I admire especially a certain prophetess who lived beside a lake in northern New York State about the year 1820. She announced to her numerous followers that she possessed the power of walking on water, and that she proposed to do so at 11 o'clock on a certain morning. At the stated time, the faithful assembled in their thousands beside the lake. She spoke to them saying: 'Are you all entirely persuaded that I can walk on water?' With one voice they replied: 'We are.' 'In that case', she announced, 'there is no need for me to do so.' And they all went home much edified.

This story lays bare an important and disturbing point about human beings, namely, that in groups which become charged with emotion they tend to relax, and even to lose for a time, the use of their critical faculties. Knowing this story lessens our surprise when we hear of an absurd notion which has a wide currency. And the more such historical accounts we know, the better equipped we are to deal intelligently with the problems and perplexities of our own age. There is, when all is said and done, very little that is new under the sun.

Citation of historical examples is also used to contrast our age with an earlier time. In 'The Menace of Old Age' Russell observes that doctors have learned how to prolong life, but have done nothing to ensure that our capacities remain at a high level in old age. Despite this failure, the populace as a whole praises the work of the doctors. In the sixteenth century a different standard prevailed: 'When Pope Adrian VI (the last non-Italian to occupy the Papal See) died a few months after his elevation, deputations of eminent Romans marched with congratulations to the house of his physician.' Such thoughts now would lead to a suit for malpractice. Russell's point, of course, is that current practice is not the unmitigated good it is often represented to be.

Russell tends to use many more historical examples than he does contemporary ones. No doubt the reason for this is that the historical stories have already stood the test of time and are unlikely to perish utterly, whereas the happenings of today will probably sink without a trace despite their seeming urgency. But his essays do occasionally mention current matters, as, for example, in 'On Economic Security' when he notes that about the only persons alive (in 1933) with a secure income were 'those Indian Princes who obtain a salary from the British Government on condition of living in Europe.' One is often astonished in reading Russell by the bewildering variety of facts with which he was acquainted. In this particular case he probably learned of this tiny class of persons from his work with Indians who sought independence for their country from British rule. Still, to have had it at the front of his mind for use in illustrating a point in an essay is remarkable. He seems never to have forgotten anything which had once come to his attention.

These essays are literally alive with allusions to his own experience. In 'On Politicians' he remarks that nearly everyone casts their votes in an election for a reason other than the superior merit of their candidate. Most when asked trace their membership of a political party to the fact that their father had belonged to it, and they readily admit that voting for that party's candidate is habitual with them. Russell cites himself in support of this observation: 'I myself, in England, vote for the Labour Party because my father was a Radical; my father was a Radical because his father was a Liberal; my grandfather was a Liberal because his father was a Whig; and he was a Whig because his ancestors obtained abbey land from Henry VIII. Having derived my radicalism from such a mercenary source, shall I turn Conservative? The very idea appals me.' In this case Russell describes himself as sharing an important characteristic with nearly everyone else. But in 'On Labelling People' he separates himself from the herd: 'When the gushing hostess says to me "Oh Mr Russell, I know you are so fond of books", I wish I could reply, with the manner of Dr Johnson, "Madam, I never read a book when some less unprofitable manner of disposing of my time is available."' In 'Are Criminals Worse than Other People?' Russell provides us with a vivid description of those he met in Brixton Prison during the six months he was confined there for opposing the First World War. The personal references in these essays constitute a series of grace notes to his autobiographical writings.

Russell was one of the wittiest writers of this century, and by their very nature these little essays provide him with an excellent opportunity to display his wit. 'Wit', as I am using the term here, is displayed in two types of remark: first, those that are clever and lively and made in an amusing way; and second, those that reveal an incongruous relationship in a surprising way. One of the most remarkable examples of a witty remark of the first type is found in *The ABC of Relativity*: 'We all have a tendency to think that the world must confirm to our prejudices. The opposite view involves some effort of thought, and most people would die sooner than think – in fact, they do so' (p. 166). Could any other writer of this century have written that? In 'On Being Good' he remarks: 'Some fool, long ago – probably a Roman – said that to know how to command, a man must first learn how to obey. This is the opposite of the truth.' Readers are bound to notice points put so provocatively. Here is an example of the second kind (with an example of the first kind thrown in for good measure): 'There is a popular notion that vegetarians are mild and gentle folk who would not hurt a fly. Perhaps they would not hurt a fly. As to this, I cannot speak, but their charity towards flies certainly does not extend to human beings. Perhaps the most powerful argument in favour of a vegetarian diet is the vigour and pugnacity which it gives to those who practise it.' It will hardly surprise the reader to learn that he called this essay 'On the Fierceness of Vegetarians.' In 'On Corporal Punishment' we find this paradigm: 'Men who, while they were schoolboys, were caned or flogged, almost invariably believe that they are the better for it. This belief itself, to my mind, is one of its bad effects.' This important observation could hardly be put more succinctly or more effectively.

As might be expected of an eminent logician, Russell often begins an essay by laying out the alternatives requiring his consideration. 'On Modern Uncertainty' opens with this witty observation: 'There have been four sorts of ages in the world's history. There have been ages when everybody thought they knew everything, ages when nobody thought they knew anything, ages when clever people thought they knew much and stupid people thought they knew little, and ages when stupid people thought they knew much and clever people thought they knew little. The first sort of age is one of stability, the second of slow decay, the third of progress, and the fourth of disaster.' In 1932 it seemed to Russell that the world was tottering into the last state, and that disaster was imminent. Scientists, economists, philosophers and statesmen all seemed unable to offer a cure for the world's troubles. 'The only people left with positive opinions are those who are too stupid to know when their opinions are absurd. Consequently the world is ruled by fools, and the intelligent count for nothing in the councils of the nations.' With the great depression deepening and a second world war looming, this gloomy assessment was not far off the mark.

An essay where his analytical skills are very much on display is 'Illegal?', which would be better named 'Should Suicide Be Illegal?'. It is Russell's only sustained discussion of suicide, which is surprising given that, by his own witness, he contemplated suicide on more than one occasion earlier in his life. In England and in most of the United States at the time he was writing both suicide and attempted suicide were illegal, positions he regarded as irrational. Suicide should not be a crime, in his opinion, since it consists of persons disposing, wisely or unwisely, of what is legally their own property, namely their lives. He arrives at this position by examining all the usual reasons given in support of the contention that suicide is a form of murder and rejecting them all. Concerning the criminality of attempted suicide he is scornful: 'When a man finds life so painful that he tries to kill himself he is given a dose of prison to teach him to find life more pleasant.' The purpose of punishment ought to be to deter, but in this case it is most unlikely to achieve its purpose.

Russell's command of the English language is truly extraordinary. He knows and employs the usual literary devices; he is especially adept at using irony to make his points. During his discussion of why teachers may not use lipstick, he remarks: 'Hypocrisy is, of course, very necessary to success in life and there is much to be said for the view that those concerned in education should be competent to teach it.' The intelligent reader (and Russell always credits his readers with more than average intelligence) nods approval of his intended meaning. Unfortunately, the literal-minded (and the stupid) form the opinion that Russell approves of hypocrisy. Clever writers do run certain risks when they allow their works to be printed and sold, especially when the subject of the work is one of social or political concern about which all readers, however unintelligent or ill-informed, consider themselves expert. On more than one occasion Russell did find himself in trouble with certain groups, and sometimes he paid a rather heavy price. But even imprisonment did not lead him to alter his writing style. Until he was a very old man he continued to delight his sympathetic readers and to provoke his detractors – as he does in these little essays – by the enormous skill with which he stated his views on the important topics of the day.

JOHN G. SLATER
University of Toronto

Contents

Contents

Preface

In the early 1930s, the *New York American* and other newspapers owned by William Randolph Hearst published a literary page to which a large number of writers and artists contributed. Among them were some distinguished authors, both English and American: Aldous Huxley, G. K. Chesterton, Havelock Ellis, V. Sackville-West, Rebecca West, Philip Wylie, James Thurber, H. L. Mencken, Gertrude Atherton, Robert Benchley, Ogden Nash, Lewis Browne, and Ludwig Lewissohn.

Bertrand Russell was one of the regulars, contributing a total of 156 essays from 22 July 1931 to 2 May 1935. In one year alone (1933), he contributed fifty items, virtually one each week.

Intended as they were for a newspaper audience, his essays made frequent reference to the events and problems of the day, the Depression, the rise of Nazism, Prohibition, the 'New Deal', and so on, but to a large extent, though many of the allusions are temporal, the themes are perennial: love, marriage, freedom, individuality, character, parenthood, peace and war, brotherhood, progress, knowledge, truth, science, ethics, education, and so on. After all, they were written by a philosopher – 'the spectator of all time and all existence,' in Plato's phrase – by one of the great minds and personalities of the twentieth century, by a man who by the end of his long and full life had pursued with vigour and even distinction five or six careers in addition to that of philosopher: mathematician, logician, educator, moralist, propagandist for social reform, and agitator for peace – and all these roles to a degree find expression in these essays.

When the essays first appeared, Lord Russell (as by then he was) was no stranger to America. He had first visited the United States in 1896 with his first wife, herself an American, staying for three months, meeting her relatives and lecturing at Bryn Mawr College and at Johns Hopkins University. He had come to the States again in 1914, 1924, 1927, 1929, and 1931.

Of all the essays which appeared during those five years in this series, only seven have ever been reprinted in a book. A few of the essays were reprinted also in certain British magazines, and one, in translation, appeared in a German magazine. This is the extent of it! By far the greater proportion of the essays have suffered the fate of yesteryear's newspaper: oblivion. They do not deserve oblivion. The publishers and I are confident that the candid and judicious reader will agree with this judgement, and it is for this reason that we make them available to a new generation of readers.

We include in the present two-volume collection all of the Hearst essays except some which dealt with transitory issues and the four which were reprinted in Russell's books during his lifetime. We are reprinting for the first time an essay ('On Being Edifying') which appeared to our knowledge only in the British journal, *Time and Tide*. We include it in this collection and also include some previously unpublished essays because they were written at about the same time as the Hearst essays and are similar to them in style and format.

Though unostentatious and sometimes even casual, the essays reveal Russell's genius: his wit, his irony, his perspicuousness, his erudition, his moral sensitivity, his boldness – why not say it? – his wisdom. Our generation has as much urgent need for his rational clarity and his sense of concern for mankind as that generation that first read the essays forty years ago. Moreover, they are a delight to read, for Russell's love of fun keeps bubbling over in them all.

I have exercised my editorial privileges lightly, supplying a few explanatory notes for the more transitory and recondite allusions here and there and indulging, in modest degree, my own prejudices relating to capitals, commas, spelling, hyphens, and the like. I have occasionally broken some of the longer sentences and paragraphs into shorter ones and *very* occasionally recast sentences to enhance clarity.

I have Mr Kenneth M. Blackwell, archivist of the Bertrand Russell Archives at McMaster University, to thank for his encouragement on this project and Barry Feinberg and Continuum 1 Ltd of London for making it a reality. I may be permitted to add that Lord Russell knew of the project and approved it, but death prevented his seeing it realised. I dedicate the volume to his revered memory.

HARRY RUJA
San Diego, California

On Jealousy

One of the dividing lines between people who are old-fashioned and people who have a modern outlook is as to jealousy. The traditional outlook was that while jealousy is to be condemned when it is unfounded, it is to be counted as just indignation where cause for it exists. Othello did wrong in murdering Desdemona because she was innocent, but if she had sinned his action would have been becoming to an officer and a gentleman. Appeals to the unwritten law are still not uncommon, and most people still view leniently a man who is driven to violence by his wife's infidelity. Indeed a tolerant attitude in such circumstances is viewed by many as unmanly.

This attitude causes jealousy to be much more violent than it need be. There is undoubtedly an instinctive element in it, but the instinctive element is greatly inflamed by the sense that one's rights are being infringed. When a man's beliefs as to his rights change, there is a corresponding change both in the violence of his jealousy and in the occasions on which he feels it. A man who in one social environment will be led by jealousy to commit murder will in another environment be led only to feel a bit surly.

Should we desire the diminution of jealousy, it can be brought about in this way. I think as regards the extreme case of the so-called unwritten law there can be no rational doubt. If a man swindles you out of your money, you may be very angry, but you are expected to seek redress through the law, not through private vengeance. It is incompatible with the whole idea of a civilised state that private wrongs should be redressed by private violence.

But what are we to say of less extreme forms of jealousy? Let it be granted that it would be better not to give grounds for jealousy, but that being admitted, we know nevertheless that many people will give such grounds. So long as jealousy is considered socially admirable, people will conceal such actions as might cause it, with the result that the most intimate of human relations becomes filled with deceit. Every man knows that he is liable to an occasional lapse from technical fidelity without on that account wishing his marriage to be broken up, but while everyone knows this concerning himself, few people can manage to believe it with regard to their partner. Everybody carries about with him two kinds of sexual psychology: one applicable to himself, the other to the person he is in love with. These two exist in watertight compartments and never meet. I believe myself that the psychology a man applies to himself is nearer to the truth than that which he applies to his wife, and I believe also that in the long run it never does any good to believe what is untrue.

I shall be told that every properly constituted man would find life intolerable if he were not absolutely convinced that his wife was more virtuous than himself, but this again depends upon expectation and social convention. The first time one learns that one's best friends are liable to be wittily satirical at one's expense, the experience is very painful, and one feels furious in spite of the consciousness of often having done the same thing oneself; but a little experience and a little reflection will convince anybody that he cannot hope to be an exception and to have none of his foibles ever laughed at. The same sort of thing applies also to graver matters.

It is possible, though I admit that it is difficult, to view oneself as no exception to general laws and as not having a sacrosanct immunity from the ordinary misfortunes of life. There is much too much pompous self-esteem in the world, and anything that diminishes the harm that people do by demanding more than their due share of the world's room is to be welcomed.

22 July 1931

Sex and Happiness

We are told that sex was inflicted upon Adam and Eve after the Fall as a punishment. From what I have seen of its workings in the present day I am inclined to agree with this view. Almost all the young men and young women that I know suffer acutely in one way or another through its workings. Can you, reader, lay your hand on your heart and say that you have derived more pleasure than pain from sex and its consequences? In the old days of masculine domination the matter was simple. Men took what they wanted, and women submitted. In this way half the human race was happy and half unhappy. But with the modern demand for justice as between men and women, this arrangement became impossible. The reformers may have intended that women should become as happy as men, but what in fact they secured was that men became as unhappy as women. All would be well if only people would pair off as they did in Victorian novels and live happily ever after. But simple and satisfactory as this prescription is, people resolutely refuse to follow it. Either the wife gets tired of the husband or the husband gets tired of the wife. If the wife is sufficiently dutiful, she may conceal the disgust inspired by her husband's habitual gestures and habitual anecdotes and habitual pronouncements on questions of public moment. In that case, she will take out her dissatisfaction on her children. Or she may seek distraction elsewhere, in which case she must either become an adept in deception or drive her husband to distraction with jealousy. If it is the husband that gets tired first, he may, if he is a man of high morality and iron self-control, take refuge in politeness and hard work, but sooner or later the strain will become intolerable, and he will either break down or break out. Sometimes the solution is sought in divorce, but the same reasons which led to the first divorce are likely to lead to a second and third. I have frequently been embarrassed in talking to American ladies to find that whatever man I happened to mention had been their husband at some time or other.

All this is very sad. It all springs, we may be told, from the mistaken notion that sex should be a source of happiness. No one changes his dentist because the hours spent in his company are not wholly pleasurable. If people expected misery from sex they would be less disappointed when they got it.

This point of view is one of respectable antiquity and is indeed bound up with much traditional morality. But is it really the best that can be done? I do not believe so: I believe that a little more realism and a little more self-control in the matter of jealousy and ill-temper would make all the difference. A great deal of our modern trouble has come from mixing up romantic love, which is a poetic and anarchic impulse, with marriage, which is a social institution. The French have not made this mistake, and on the whole they are considerably happier in these respects than the English-speaking nations.

However that may be, it is clear that precept and practice in our day are in some way at fault. Modern marriage too often fails not only to give happiness to the husband and wife but also to produce satisfactory children, which is its purpose considered as an institution. The children of modern marriages are apt to be few, nervous, and over-wrought, surrounded by an atmosphere of anxiety in which it is impossible for them to thrive, either neglected by their mothers or watched with too meticulous a solicitude. Somehow or other, the old institutions seem to be out of gear. It is useless to preach that men and women ought to return to the modes of behaviour of a simpler age, for they will not do it. An ethic is called for, but it must be a new ethic, and above all it must be realistic in taking account of the facts as they exist in our day.

5 August 1931

Tourists

We Lose Our Charm Away from Home

It is an odd fact that, while we are all charming people when we are at home, most of us become horrid as soon as we travel abroad. English travellers in the United States frequently have made me blush by their arrogance, their wholly unfounded superciliousness and their blindness to the very important merits of American civilisation.

This foolish behaviour causes untravelled Americans to think far worse of the English than they deserve. The fact is that the average tourist, of whatever nation, views the life of a foreign country in its more trivial aspects and fails to display his own best qualities. This applies not only to European tourists but also to those from the Western Hemisphere, with the result that Europeans who have never left their own continent get a very false impression of Americans.

Speaking broadly and ignoring many exceptions, one may say that Americans come to Europe chiefly to find satisfaction for those parts of human nature which are least catered to in their own country. A degenerate Italian aristocrat with a name familiar in Renaissance history is more interesting to these Americans than Einstein. To Europeans, unless they are professional antiquaries, such an attitude is impossible, since they have to live in the present and, if possible, make Europe fit to live in. Nor do they observe that American interest in European historical survivals always is very discriminating.

A culture impregnated with history has a certain depth and solidity which may not be without value; but the mere survival of quaint costumes, titles and customs has only the superficial kind of interest that is exploited by Hollywood. No one likes to be the object of this kind of interest, and Europeans tend to be impatient of being regarded as picturesque though absurd relics.

There is another, less cultivated tourist, who seeks, chiefly in Paris, a loosening of the moral restraints to which he is subject when at home. He does not suspect that the Parisians have their own code and therefore does not know when he offends against it. But throughout his enjoyment the serious aspects of French life remain hidden from him.

It is a curious feature of American (and to some extent of British) civilisation that those who have created and maintained it seek for themselves, in their spare time, something differing from it as widely as possible. This does not apply, for example, to the civilisation of France. A Frenchman likes a foreign country in proportion as it resembles his own, and there is no feature of his own world from which he longs to escape. What is the reason for this difference?

My explanation is that the French have been thinking mainly of what was agreeable to themselves; while many Americans, and not a few British, under the influence of their lofty ethical standards, have been thinking mainly of what would be good for their neighbours. What is good for us is, alas, not always agreeable, though it is gratifying to think that we are producing what is good for others. Consequently the pleasure to be derived from American civilisation largely is the altruistic pleasure of reflecting upon the noble men and women it is producing, while for private delight countries based upon a less exalted morality are more agreeable. This is, I believe, the explanation of the curious paradox that even the most patriotic Americans seek out eagerly whatever is most different from what they approve in their own country.

24 August 1931

The Menace of Old Age

One of the greatest perils of our time has crept upon us almost unobserved. The skill of the medical profession has prolonged the span of human life but has not yet learned to prolong the span of human capacity. Throughout the last sixty years people have been getting born less and less and have also died less and less. The result is that the average age of the population is continually increasing. Strange to say, the doctors who produce this result by skilful ministration to their aged patients are thought to deserve well of the public. When Pope Adrian VI (the last non-Italian to occupy the Papal See) died a few months after his elevation, deputations of eminent Romans marched with congratulations to the house of his physician. But this spirit, alas, has died out.

The results of this unfortunate misdirection of scientific ability are already becoming apparent. I have the misfortune to live in a country whose government is composed almost entirely of men over seventy.[1] There were originally several younger men, but they resigned; of those who remain several have been known to me for thirty or forty years. I can remember a period when they had vigour and initiative; there was a time when it seemed to them quite natural to act in accordance with their beliefs. But there is no standing up to physiology. As our tissues stiffen, our habits become more set: we go through the same motions every day (I am speaking as an old man) when we shave, when we brush our hair, or when we relate our favourite anecdote. We may remain intellectually convinced of the necessity of change since this is one of our fixed verbal habits, but we cannot bear actual change. The aged radical is therefore in the sad situation that he can only be happy so long as he is ineffective; he cannot stop doing any of the things that he always has done, including the advocacy of change, but not of course including its actual realisation.

One of the saddest cases known to me was that of the secretary of the Society for Legalising Marriage with a Deceased Wife's Sister. He obtained this post as a vigorous young man of twenty-two. Through his untiring efforts and by the exercise of immense skill, he succeeded in the course of fifty years in converting the British public to the necessity of the reform which this society advocated. The measure once passed, the society was no longer needed, and he lost his job. By this time he was an old man of seventy-two, capable of only one thing, namely, the clear and vigorous statement of the arguments for a measure which had already been passed. (I do not vouch for the above facts, but it is quite likely that something of the sort occurred.)

Most old men have the good sense to avoid this sad fate and to do what they can to prevent even those changes in the environment which they have always advocated. Consequently every increase in medical skill is bound to make the world more and more conservative. Probably in another hundred years most people will be over eighty. They will be doddering, mumbling, and altogether senile, but rich, respected, and powerful. They will hold all the important posts in spite of the eagerness of young men of sixty to replace them.

In such a world all progress will be impossible. What is to be done about it? Swift, who foresaw the danger, suggested that at the age of eighty a man suspected of undue longevity should be deprived of his vote and his property. This is an admirable suggestion, but already the old men have so firm a hold of power that I am afraid Swift's plan is not practical politics. I suggest that all medical men under sixty should band themselves together into a league for the defence of youth and that they should exert their influence to prevent all researches calculated to prolong the life of the very old. By the threat of such a movement, the old may be induced to surrender their power. Once robbed of their power, they might become objects of benevolence. I would have them transported to islands in the South Seas, where there should be no prohibition and a plentiful supply of cigars and where special newspapers should be published under a strict censorship with orders to represent that the world is going to the dogs and that in no respect is any improvement occurring anywhere. By this means happiness could be brought to the declining years of these victims of medical skill without their being in a position to oppress the young or to prevent the world from adjusting itself to new conditions.

27 August 1931

In Praise of Artificiality

Mankind is divided into two classes: those who, being artificial, praise nature, and those who, being natural, praise art. The praise of nature, in which our age abounds, is not itself natural: it is a reaction against too much artificiality. As a reaction, it has its uses; as a theory of life, it won't do.

I once watched a raven and his mate having a meal. The meal consisted of raw flesh, some of it tender, some of it tough. The male bird first ate all the tender portions, administering savage pecks to the female if she dared to approach. It was only when nothing fit to eat remained that the female was allowed to appease her appetite as best she might. I was led to consider what human meals would be like if they were conducted in this fashion. From the point of view of vigorous young men the result might be quite agreeable, but for women, children and old men the rules of polite behaviour are more advantageous.

All civilisation, especially on its aesthetic side, is artificial. Manners, good speech, good writing, good music, good dancing – everything that gives grace to life depends, not upon the denial of natural impulses, but upon training them to express themselves in ways that are delightful rather than in ways that are crude.

I visited yesterday a brand-new little restaurant on the coast of Spain. It existed almost entirely for the supply of drinks. The manager, a gay and charming young man, had spent his leisure moments painting delicious but very artificial pictures on the walls. His especial pride was in two ships, a French one being struck by lightning and a Spanish one sailing on serenely. He was a civilised being and tended to civilise his clientele because he made drinking artificial and stylistic, not a mere quenching of gross thirst.

Under the influence of the gospel of work, the northern nations have lost the graces which still survive, though precariously, in the south. The gospel of work teaches men that what matters is the resulting product, not the style displayed during its production. We build houses without beauty in which we eat meals that merely nourish, and beget children without love whom we subject to an education that destroys spontaneity and grace. Where there is delight in a process, there will be style, and the activity of production will itself have aesthetic quality. But when men assimilate themselves to machines and value only the consequences of their work, not the work itself, style disappears, to be replaced by something which to the mechanised man appears more natural, though in fact it is only more brutal.

Is this misfortune inevitable as men become more mechanised? I do not think so. We have allowed ourselves to be too much dominated by work and have not sufficiently used machines as a means of liberation from the thraldom of manual and mental labour. We could, if we chose, all have more leisure. We could, if we chose, educate our children so as to enable them to give artistic expression to their impulses, rather than so as to be convenient units in a regiment. We do not do this because we love power more than we love beauty. But I doubt whether the exclusive pursuit of power is the best road to happiness. Human nature contains other ingredients, which are at least equally worthy to be honoured. Until the machine age learns to give them their due place, the new civilisation will not be completely sane.

9 September 1931

Who May Use Lipstick?

'What a silly question!' the reader may say. 'Of course, every woman uses lipstick nowadays.' But a little reflection shows that there are still some kinds of women to whom this otherwise universal toleration is not extended. Perhaps if we consider who the women are who are not allowed to use lipstick we shall get an interesting sidelight upon conventional ideas of ethical merit.

Female ministers of religion, while they should be neat in their person, should not have any such adornments as may be supposed calculated to attract the male sex, unless they hail from Southern California. While they are engaged in exhorting us to a life of self-denial, there should be no obvious sign that they do not practise what they preach. Welfare workers should not employ lipstick, in spite of the fact that all the ladies from whom their funds come do so. Hospital nurses while on duty must appear to have no interest except the health of their patients, and the Sister in charge would certainly reproach them if they were found unduly beautified during the hours of work.

The largest class of victims of this curious taboo are teachers. I do not know how it may be in America, but in England any female teacher who wishes to be not unattractive gets into hot water.

Let us try for a moment to think out the philosophy underlying these restrictions. In the first place, it is held – and so far we may agree – that a teacher should have a good moral influence; in the second place, it is held that no woman can have a good moral influence unless she is or pretends to be indifferent to the male sex. In a young woman this implies either hypocrisy or psychological ill-health.

Hypocrisy is, of course, very necessary to success in life and there is much to be said for the view that those concerned in education should be competent to teach it. I do not think, however, that those who enforce this restriction upon teachers are intending to demand hypocrisy: they consider that the sort of woman who is capable of being a good teacher must be genuinely indifferent on the subject of her own attractions.

For my part I think this view profoundly mistaken. Unless there is physical ill-health, indifference to the opposite sex on the part of a young person can only be secured by means of somewhat violent repressions, which will inevitably produce an attitude of severity and discipline very inimical to the happy and spontaneous development of children.

It is generally admitted that most grown-up people, however regrettably, will try to have a good time, but it is felt that the whole weight of authority should be directed to teaching children that virtue is unpleasant, on the ground, apparently, that this is the way to make them love virtue. In order to prove to them that virtue is unpleasant, education authorities try to provide teachers who shall be at once unpleasant and virtuous.

For my part I have a different view as to the best sort of person. I think people should be jolly, and cheerful, and kindly, and more inclined to say 'Yes' than to say 'No'; those who say 'No' to themselves generally feel that this gives them a right to say 'No' to others, especially to children.

For this reason I think it important that jollity should not be thought a crime in those whose profession it is to be in contact with the young, and generally in those whose business it is to uphold moral standards.

14 September 1931

The Lessons of Experience

It is a commonplace that the young are influenced by imagination and reasoning while the old are guided by experience. When I myself was young I had once a remarkable illustration of this fact. I had walked from the old-world village of Clovelly, in Devonshire, to a cape called Hartland Point, from which I could see Lundy Island at the mouth of the Bristol Channel. I got into conversation with a coast guard, who told me that the distance to Clovelly was eight miles, and to Lundy Island ten miles. 'And how far is it from Clovelly to Lundy Island?' I asked. The answer was twenty-two miles. At this I burst out into argument to the effect that two sides of a triangle are always greater than the third side, and that if one went by way of Hartland Point the distance would only be eighteen miles. The coast guard, however, was quite unmoved. 'All I can say, sir,' he replied, 'is that I was speaking with Captain Jones the other day, and he said: "I've known this coast, man and boy, for thirty years, and I make it twenty-two miles." ' Before the man-and-boy argument, geometry had to retire abashed.

This story has a moral. The government of the world, moral as well as political, is almost wholly in the hands of the old, who have known the world, 'man and boy', not merely for thirty years, but for fifty, sixty, or seventy. All these men have learnt from experience to believe what they already believed before they had experience, for most people learn nothing from experience, except confirmation of their prejudices. To learn anything genuinely from experience requires a kind of open-mindedness which is the essence of the scientific temper, though many men of science are somewhat lacking in it. Science, while it is based upon experience, enables us to anticipate experience and to know many things better than they can be known from the 'man-and-boy' type of experience.

The world is very largely what we make of it. Our theories

mould the world and may become true by being believed. In a different society, where other beliefs prevail, the world will seem quite different. Therefore, even if your prejudices are confirmed by your experience, it may be that a different experience would have confirmed a quite different set of prejudices. Schopenhauer died of taking a bath, having never tried one till an advanced age. This confirmed his friends' prejudices.

The chief superiority of America to western Europe is that the 'man-and-boy' type of argument has less force there than in more traditional countries. Eastern Europe and northern Asia have lately become untraditional, with what results it is as yet difficult to judge. But western Europe goes on in the old way in a new world, and is perishing from the intensity of its belief in the value of experience. This applies to business methods, political methods, educational methods, methods of building houses, indeed to almost everything except scientific theory, in which, oddly enough, western Europe remains supreme. But scientific theory is known only to a small aristocracy of intellect and touches ordinary social life only through the technique to which it leads. And every new technique is hateful to traditionalists. Generals are expected to be able to ride and are represented on horseback when statues are put up to them, although in war no modern general has time to career about on a horse. A modern-minded government would make statues of its generals in motor cars.

23 September 1931

Hope and Fear

In the life of every man there are some elements that are practically inalterable while there are others which are subject to fluctuations, fortunate or unfortunate. The inalterable elements are taken for granted while those that fluctuate are matters for hope and fear. The character of a man's emotional life is therefore intimately dependent upon the social system under which he lives, since his emotions will be directed toward what is doubtful rather than toward what is certain. If a man's income is fixed, he will not think much about money; if his social position is inalterable, he will not be a snob; if he believes his country's greatness to be unassailable, he will not be a vehement nationalist.

To take another set of values: if a man believes himself incurably stupid, he will not have intellectual ambitions; if he knows that he has no aesthetic sense, he will not seek artistic distinction; if he is aware of being incurably commonplace, he will not live for fame.

In the modern world (outside Russia) income and social position are more fluctuating, on the average, than they have ever previously been.

A man may make a million by speculation one year and lose it all in the following year. While he possesses his million he has a good social position; when he loses it, he has none. Without taking such an extreme case, most people, throughout the Western world, are considerably poorer now than they were two years ago; in good times, conversely, most people grow richer.

The result of this uncertainty is that men are more preoccupied about money than they ever were. In former days, this preoccupation was confined to a small minority, whereas now it is almost universal. As a natural consequence of the economic uncertainty, men have come to be admired in proportion to their success in the scramble. Few stand aside, and those who do are not respected, since it is thought that they do so from timorousness, not because they value other things more than much money.

The ideal of financial success is set before the young by most of the influences that form their minds. In the cinema they see representations of luxury, where plutocrats own marble halls and beautiful ladies in splendid dresses. The hero generally succeeds, in the end, in belonging to this successful class. Even artists come to be judged by the amount of money they make. Merit not measured in money comes to be despised. Every kind of sensitiveness, being a handicap in the struggle, is regarded as a stigma of failure.

A hundred years ago the rich arrived at the possession of a certain amount of education and culture, without which they could not be respected. Nowadays education and culture are becoming more and more confined to teachers and professors, who are despised for being poor. The level of the rich in this respect has therefore very greatly deteriorated in recent times.

It is unlikely that this loss to civilisation can be made good without a change in our social system. But it is important that the loss should be realised, since its existence is one of the reasons for thinking our present world not wholly perfect. A world in which a man is unlikely to lose his financial standing and cannot easily improve it will be a world where other than monetary values will have weight.

If, therefore, we wish to diminish the love of money which, we are told, is the root of all evil, the first step must be the creation of a system in which everyone has enough and no one has too much.

7 October 1931

Are Criminals Worse than Other People?

One of the most annoying things about the modern world is that it is so much less simple than it used to be. The world used to be divided sharply into honest men and rogues; honest men kept the law, rogues broke it. Rogues, though they might prosper for a while, invariably came to a bad end; some honest men might fail to become rich, but this was considered exceptional, as was shown by the phrase 'honest though poor'.

In such a world no one suffered from the doubts and hesitations and the blurring of sharp lines which cause modern men to vacillate. A long course of rebellious writers has tried to persuade us that it is the wicked who prosper and that the rich, even if they do break the law, are not at all likely to be punished for doing so. Every student of history or sociology must be struck by the fact that the men who do the most harm are not the sort of criminals who are sent to prison but the sort to whom equestrian statues are put up. And so one is led to ask oneself in all seriousness: are criminals any worse than other people? And if not, what is the peculiarity which leads to their being sent to prison?

There was a period during the war when I associated habitually with criminals.[2] I cannot say that I found anything peculiarly dislikeable about them. They fell into various classes. There were debtors who had been ordered by a judge to pay more than they possessed and had therefore been sent to prison for contempt of court. There was a rich, blind lawyer, seventy years of age, who had gone to gaol for bigamy. There was a fine, upstanding soldier who had been sentenced with what he thought undue severity for returning five minutes late from leave and had thereupon vowed that he would not do another hand's turn of fighting for the authorities: in order to keep this vow, he had made a point of stealing whisky whenever he was released from prison, which, however, occurred with increasing rarity. Then there was a fat, cheerful, good-natured fellow, who was a connoisseur in prisons and always chose his gaol with care; his reason for a criminal career was that only in prison could he escape from his wife. Then there was a man who had been for seventeen years an officer of the Salvation Army, whose boy had been fined for coming late to school; the Salvationist considered that the fine had been inflicted from malice and therefore refused to pay it; he was, however, persuaded that the Lord had led him to that place for a wise purpose. In addition to these desperate ruffians, there were three members of the Soviet Government and a large number of men who considered it their duty to obey the precepts of the Sermon on the Mount.[3] On the whole, the people I met in prison seemed to me more agreeable companions than the members of the best clubs.

There are, however, two types of criminals who certainly are undesirable: they are the men who are exceptionally violent and the men who are exceptionally cunning. Murderers and forgers may be taken as representing these two types. In the case of the murderer there is, of course, an element of bad luck; almost anybody might become a murderer given sufficient provocation, but most of us have the good fortune never to be sufficiently provoked. Men differ greatly, however, as regards the degree of provocation necessary to lead them to crimes of violence. Ungovernable rage is a psychological aberration and should be treated by the psychiatrist; it is a mark of disease rather than of wickedness.

The forger and the fraudulent company promoter belong to a different category; they differ from other men chiefly by the fact that they are more optimistic; they take the chance of detection more readily than other men because temperamentally they overestimate the probabilities in their favour. This is attributable partly to an education in boosting[4] and partly to unduly healthy glands. The treatment to which they should be subjected is a course of Schopenhauer and lobster salad, to cure them simultaneously of optimism and good digestion.

To prevent crime there are therefore two requisites: one is to make crime contrary to self-interest, and this is a matter for the criminal law and the police; the other is to give men that degree of self-control and sound judgement which will enable them to act in accordance with their own interests – this is a matter for the psychologist. But in neither department has the moralist anything useful to contribute.

29 October 1931

The Advantages of Cowardice

During the French Revolution, when the Reign of Terror came to an end, it was found that no one was left alive among the politicians except prudent cowards who had changed their opinions quickly enough to keep their heads on their shoulders. The result was twenty years of military glory, because there was no one left among the politicians with sufficient courage to keep the generals in order. The French Revolution was an exceptional time, but wherever organisation exists cowardice will be found more advantageous than courage. Of the men at the head of businesses, schools, lunatic asylums, and the like, nine out of ten will prefer the supple lickspittle to the outspoken man of independent judgement. In politics it is necessary to profess the party programme and flatter the leaders; in the navy it is necessary to profess antiquated views on naval strategy; in the army it is necessary to maintain a mediaeval outlook on everything; in journalism wage slaves have to use their brains to give expression to the opinions of millionaires; in education professors lose their jobs if they do not respect the prejudices of the illiterate.

The result of this state of affairs is that in practically every walk of life the men who come to the top have served a long apprenticeship in cowardice, while the honest and courageous have to be sought for in workhouses and prisons. Is this regrettable?

The modern world, owing to industrialism, requires social co-operation more than it was required in any earlier stage in the world's history. Now there are three reasons for which you may co-operate with a man: because you love him, because you fear him, or because you hope to share the swag. These three motives are of differing importance in different regions of human co-operation: the first governs procreation, and the third governs politics. But the ordinary everyday business of government, whether in the state or in any other social institution, depends upon fear. A collection of fearless men would be ungovernable. The Vikings were men whom the King of Norway found ungovernable; they left Norway because they would not submit themselves to his sway. After a few centuries of adventure, they became peasants in the frozen valleys of Iceland.

Consider, as a contrast, the great Duke of Marlborough. He secured the first steps in his career by causing his sister to become the mistress of James II. His great days were due to the passionate friendship between his wife and Queen Anne. Whenever he fought the French he beat them, but he was always ready to refrain from fighting if the King of France made it worth his while. He left a great name, and a great fortune, and his descendants to this day are patterns for patriots. The arts of success have changed little since his day, in spite of the nominal advent of democracy. Now, as in the past, if you wish for success you should be insinuating and pusillanimous rather than bold and self-reliant.

To those, therefore, whose ambition it is to die in the odour of sanctity, respected by bank managers, admired by friends and neighbours, and universally regarded as models of what a citizen should be, my advice is: don't express your own opinions but those of your boss; don't endeavour to realise ends which you yourself think good, but pursue rather those aimed at by some organisation supported by millionaires; in your private friendships select influential men if you can, or, failing that, men whom you judge likely to become influential. Do this, and you will win the good opinion of all the best elements in the community.

This is sound advice, but, for my part, I would sooner die than follow it.

2 November 1931

The Decay of Meditation

A hundred years ago and, still more, a hundred and fifty years ago, well-to-do people, though less numerous than they are now, were certainly more civilised. A rich man, in those days, was expected to be able to quote the Latin poets, to judge Italian Renaissance pictures, and to appreciate classical music. He had, as a rule, a considerable knowledge of the literature of his own country and (even if he were not French) of that of France.

Nowadays, such erudition is only expected of professors, and then only in departments – one professor knows Latin, another knows the old masters, another knows music, and yet another knows whatever is least worth knowing in modern literature. The rich would think it beneath their dignity to have such knowledge, and ignorance has become the hallmark of social eminence.

All this is perhaps not very serious. I have found few occasions in life when it was necessary to know the names of the Muses or the signs of the Zodiac, both of which were taught to my grandmothers in childhood and still remembered at the age of eighty.

In the modern world there is hardly any leisure, not because men work harder than they did, but because their pleasures have become as strenuous as their work. The result is that, while cleverness has increased, wisdom has decreased because no one has time for the slow thoughts out of which wisdom, drop by drop, is distilled. A problem such as the prevention of war, the urgency of which is obvious to every one, is dismissed with a shrug of the shoulders in the hope that circumstances will solve it without the aid of human thought. But circumstances, unaided, are not likely to be so kind.

This result, paradoxically enough, has been brought about by time-saving devices. Take, for example, locomotion. The faster people can travel, the more time they spend travelling. Now they go by train and take about an hour from house to office. The same sort of thing applies to visiting: formerly one visited only such neighbours as one's horses could reach without undue fatigue, whereas now one can visit anywhere within a hundred miles.

Or again, take the telephone. I once had a long-distance conversation with a deaf old gentleman who had rung me up. I said, 'It's Bertrand Russell speaking.' He said, 'What?' I repeated my statement more loudly, but he again said, 'What?' At last, by nearly bursting my lungs, I made him hear, and he replied, 'Why, I knew that.' There was no time for further conversation. A useful invention, the telephone.

The accumulation of such futilities fills busy days and gives a wholly fictitious impression of work done. Quakers, who retain more wisdom than most moderns, owe it, I believe, largely to their practice of silent meditation. If we spent half an hour every day in silent immobility, I am convinced that we should conduct all our affairs, personal, national, and international, far more sanely than we do at present.

Two minutes a year, on Armistice Day, are given to silence, and all the other minutes of the year to largely futile bustle. The proportion is wrong; if the silence were longer, the bustle would be less futile.

4 November 1931

Marriage

A few days ago in a taxi in New York, the driver turned around (to the risk of our lives) and said: 'Excuse me, are you Bertrand Russell?'

I saw that denial would be useless, so I admitted the fact. He then went on to say that in former days he had heard me lecture, but that belonged to his intellectual past. 'Now,' he continued, 'I am a married man and have ceased to be a person.'

This seemed a painful result of matrimony and naturally set me reflecting. Why should marriage, which ought to be the fulfilment of personality, be felt as quite the opposite? There was no suggestion that his marriage was unhappy; it was to marriage as such that he attributed this dire result. I never myself experienced any such result of being married, but I know that the taxi driver was putting into words what a great many people feel.

The reason lies partly in economics, partly in social custom. The latter, as being easier to set right, I will consider first.

The convention that husbands and wives should spend their leisure hours together is a bad one. No doubt my taxi driver's wife does not care for lectures and also does not like him to go to them without her. Many husbands and many wives will forgo their own pleasures out of jealousy of the pleasures that they imagine their partners as desiring. It is much more harmful to object to other people's pleasures than it is to be a trifle selfish in pursuing one's own, and a certain amount of social separateness of husband and wife is necessary if they are not to become dull and incapable of finding anything to say to each other. In this respect, however, a better convention is rapidly spreading.

The economic difficulty is more serious. An unmarried man can take liberties with his income that a married man cannot take. No doubt most unmarried men devote their leisure to mere amusement, including the search for a wife.

But there are a certain proportion who seek the kind of education for which there is no remuneration in dollars and cents. These men, when they marry, find that their leisure is gone and that, even if they had leisure, they have no spare cash. Women who are what, in a woman, is called 'intellectual' feel this loss in marriage much more than men do, unless they remain childless. The result is a certain feeling against marriage on the part of both men and women.

This trouble cannot be wholly cured unless and until the state undertakes the whole expense of children, which is not likely to happen in our time. But a good deal can be done to mitigate it by a more intelligent attitude toward the rearing of infants than that which was universal in the past and is still too frequent.

The rearing of children is a matter calling for a great deal of skill and science and giving scope for much interesting observation. No amount of skill and science can replace affection, but it can and should supplement affection, which, when it is ill-informed, may produce effects precisely contrary to those that were intended. I believe that, as people come to realise the scientific interest of infancy, intellectuals will grow less superior about family life.

The ignorant person with affection is perhaps better for an infant than a well-informed person who has no heart; but a well-informed person who is fond of children is much better than either.

13 November 1931

On Being Good

Everybody who has much to do with boys comes, in time, to prefer the boy who is sometimes 'bad' to the boy who is invariably 'good'. The boy who fills the master's desk with frogs, puts mice in the way of the maids, steals the apples in the orchard before they are ripe and absents himself from class when there is a circus is a 'bad' boy and is likely to be frequently punished, though such punishment is merely a conventional folly. But in the very moment of punishing him any sensible schoolmaster will prefer him to the 'good' boy who obeys every precept to the letter and always says 'yes, sir', or 'no, sir', as circumstances demand.

We believe a boy ought to show spirit and should on occasion have the pluck to defy the authorities and take the consequences. At any rate, this is the belief where the sons of the well-to-do are concerned; courage in wage-earners is less admired by the authorities.

The adult world is growing less and less suitable to the qualities of the 'bad' boy. Nelson was a bad boy to the end of his days; so was Julius Caesar. But nowadays almost every young man has to begin with a very subordinate post in some vast organisation. His superiors seldom have the tolerance of the experienced schoolmaster and are likely to give promotion to the 'good' boy.

Unfortunately docility is not a quality which is often found in the man capable of initiative or leadership. Some fool, long ago – probably a Roman – said that to know how to command, a man must first learn how to obey. This is the opposite of the truth. The man who has learnt to obey will either have lost all personal initiative or will have become so filled with rage against the authorities that his initiative will have become destructive and cruel.

It seldom happens, therefore, that the best men rise to the top. In the great majority of cases they will have proved themselves so insubordinate or so critical of their superiors that they will have ceased to form part of any powerful organisation.

One may take the political machine as an illustration. It is an odd fact that, in a democracy, where the eminent politicians are chosen by the people, there is almost everywhere a general agreement that politicians are a poor lot, so much so that the very word 'politician' has acquired a flavour of contempt. The chief reason for this state of affairs, I should say, is to be found in the rigidity of party discipline. A party has, at any given moment, a set of opinions and policies which must be adhered to by all its active members, however little they may agree at heart. Orthodoxy is more valued than either honesty or acumen, with the result that most young men who are not mediocre find the whole business intolerable and abandon it before they have had a chance to become leaders.

Since organisation is inevitable in the modern world, there is no way out of this trouble except to imbue the men in important positions with toleration for the vagaries of the young. When men have already become important there is, of course, no hope of improving them, since they will no longer listen to advice. Unfortunately, the improvement of the young is generally left to those who have already become old and important. I can only suggest that no school should have a head more than thirty years of age. But I hardly expect to see this admirable reform adopted.

18 November 1931

Who Gets Our Savings?

During the last two years, in every quarter of the globe, men who had saved money throughout a long and laborious life found themselves suddenly and unexpectedly poor. 'Poor' is, of course, a relative term. I met a business man in California who told me a hard luck story about a friend of his who, after following all the best precepts, was left in his old age with a mere $40,000 a year. To any European this seems like wealth beyond the dreams of avarice, but in California it is considered little removed from beggary.

Whatever may be the standard of life in different parts of the world, all are alike in the fact that almost everybody has become poorer. Wage earners have had their wages cut and investors have found their investments becoming worthless.

Where has all the money gone? When a man picks my pocket, the money goes to him, and I have at least the consolation (or what would be such if I were truly virtuous) of thinking that the pickpocket's children will get a good Christmas dinner. But when a concern in which I have invested goes bankrupt, the money vanishes into thin air, and in many cases no one is the richer. Sometimes, of course, a competitor benefits, but in the majority of cases there is sheer loss without compensating gain to any one.

I spent the summer at a seaside resort where an attempt had been made to enlarge the area of available building land by reclaiming a considerable region from the sea. After some years of work, spring tides proved that the project was not feasible and all the money that had been spent was as completely lost as if it had been thrown into deep water.

This case illustrates, on a small scale, what has been happening throughout the world. Sometimes through one form of folly, sometimes through another, the men who direct the business enterprises of mankind have landed themselves and their followers in disaster. It is odd that, in spite of this, the survivors continue to inspire just as much awe and reverence as before.

Depressions such as the one through which the world is now passing do not have natural causes lying beyond human control. They are the result solely of human stupidity and lack of organisation. One country has too much gold, another has too little.

America lends money to England, England lends it to Germany, Germany becomes nearly bankrupt in the attempt to pay it back in reparations to England and France, who spend it on armaments intended to compel Germany to go on paying. To such a system there is no conclusion except organised slaughter, in which whatever wealth may exist at the beginning will be destroyed.

The causes of our troubles are stupidity and competition, especially competition between nations in the form of war and armaments. It is doubtful whether we shall be able to emerge into real prosperity without a great deal more international economic organisation than we have at present.

Means ought to exist by which investors could obtain impartial and well-informed advice not only as to particular investments but as to general tendencies. As the world grows more complex and the mechanism of production more difficult to understand, it becomes increasingly difficult for the private citizen to form a sound judgement as to how to get the best return for his money.

Unless some way can be found of avoiding such losses as have occurred during the last two years, the habit of saving will die out and we shall spend all we earn on immediate pleasures. Every one will have a short life and a merry one, but civilisation will go to the wall.

1 December 1931

Children

It is commonly supposed that all parents, except a few unnatural wretches, love their children. In theory, perhaps, they do, but in practice the love too often shows itself only in slaps and cross reproofs. Whatever the child does is wrong: he must not talk, he must not fidget, he must not roll down a grassy bank in the park. The only thing he may do without getting into trouble is to sit still and wish he were dead.

This is when his parents are untouched by modern child psychology, as the great majority still are. When parents have learnt the new catchwords, the only result is that the situation is reversed; it is now the parent who must suffer in silence while the child is allowed to make himself a nuisance. The modern parent is conscientious, but is not on that account any more instinctively fond of her child than the old-fashioned parent who finds relief for irritation in physical chastisement. Nevertheless, both struggle on, because sentimentality has decreed that there is no joy equal to that to be derived from the companionship between children and parents.

This trouble is caused by failure to recognise a very simple fact, namely, that, at all ages beyond the second birthday, people prefer the society of their contemporaries to that of people much older or younger than themselves. Men and women between the ages of twenty and thirty do not enjoy the company of old people of seventy. Women of sixty do not wish to be perpetually accompanied by girls of nineteen. But in the case of parents and children this rule is ignored, although it is quite as true as in any other case. The causes of this are physiological; children need constant movement and almost constant noise, whereas adults need rest for muscles and nerves.

The home may have been a perfect environment for the child when the home was a farm in the country and the child was one of ten. But when the home is a small urban apartment and the child has at most one brother or sister, the matter is otherwise. In that case, while children and parents are likely to love one another if they are apart most of the day, they will be perpetually on each other's nerves if they have to be cooped up together from morning till night. The resulting friction is irritating to parents and disastrous to children.

The schools of all civilised countries are still based upon the entirely antiquated notion that the most important part of education is the acquisition of knowledge. The state takes enormous pains to cause its juvenile citizens to know the multiplication table and what happened in 1776.

Far be it from me to decry such accomplishments, but the training of character seems to me of even greater importance. Now character is mainly determined before the age of six, when schooling begins. If the state understood modern child psychology it would make all children go to nursery school from the age of two onward.

There the child would find an environment composed of other children, with a grown-up in the background who would unobtrusively give a sense of safety. There would be no prohibition of noise and movement; there would be a minimum of dangers to be guarded against; and there would be as few things forbidden as a carefully arranged environment would make possible.

In the evening the children would return home, their parents would love them and they would love their parents, and all would be well. Even the fondest wife is glad that her husband is out at business most of the day, and mothers have need of relief quite as much as wives.

11 December 1931

On Politicians

It is a curious fact that the more democratic a country becomes, the less respect it has for its rulers. Aristocracies and foreign conquerors may be hated but they are not despised. Nations which select the men who are to govern them might have been expected to choose men commanding universal admiration and affection; it might have been thought that those who were deemed wisest and best would be selected for the delicate and responsible job of managing other people's affairs.

This, however, is not the case. In most democratic countries to call a man a politician is to say something derisive about him. The men who enjoy the good opinion of the community, with few exceptions, do not seek to win its votes and would be unsuccessful if they did, while the men who win votes are apt to be professionals of a not wholly admirable kind. (I am not thinking of those who obtain the highest offices.)

This is a paradox which was not foreseen by the pioneers of democracy. Indeed, it was not true in their day. When democracy is new it usually brings great men to the fore but it loses this merit as it becomes well established. Why is this?

Everybody is ready with the answer: It is due to the machine. But this is only half an answer since it does not tell us why we all submit to the machine. Why is it that, if Satan and Beelzebub were nominated as the official candidates and the Archangel Gabriel stood as an independent, the Archangel would have no chance of being elected? For that is the fact, strange as it may seem.

One reason is that an independent candidate does not command such large campaign funds and therefore cannot generate mass enthusiasm by the techniques in which politicians are adepts. But this reason, again, does not take us all the way, since it leaves us wondering why men are so unwilling to subscribe to the campaign funds of independents. The answer, no doubt, is that independents are not likely to be elected, which is also a reason for not voting for them. But that only brings us back to our first question: why are they not likely to be elected?

The ultimate reason, I believe, is nothing more recondite than habit. Most men, without inquiring into the merits of the particular candidate, vote as they always have voted, and always have voted as their fathers always voted. This applies to reformers just as much as to conservatives.

I myself, in England, vote for the Labour Party because my father was a Radical; my father was a Radical because his father was a Liberal; my grandfather was a Liberal because his father was a Whig; and he was a Whig because his ancestors obtained abbey land from Henry VIII.

Having derived my radicalism from such a mercenary source, shall I turn Conservative? The very idea appals me. No one can free himself from the force of habit, and if he could he would be reduced to such a condition of doubt that he would achieve nothing. Yet so long as habit holds sway, good men will have little chance in politics.

Is there, then, no solution? Yes, but it is a matter of degree; we must be dominated by habit to some extent but we might be less so than we are. And that lessening might make all the difference. Meanwhile, let us remember that in a democracy criticism of our politicians is criticism of ourselves – we have the politicians we deserve.

16 December 1931

Keeping Pace?

From the Stone Age to the present day, the rapidity of human progress has been gradually increasing. If a cave man could have returned to Egypt somewhere about the year 4000 BC he would have felt that the hurry of modern life had become almost unbearable. Men were altering their habits, taking to agriculture instead of hunting, and doing strange things with metals instead of being content with flints like their ancestors. This sort of thing, he would have said, must stop; the younger generation is becoming altogether too uppish.

Nevertheless it did not stop; on the contrary, except for the interval for recuperation during the Dark Ages, men have not merely continued to progress, but have progressed with continually increasing speed.

Is there any natural limit to this process? I think probably that the limit is to be found in the human nervous system. Children are born with essentially the same nervous system as belonged to children in the Stone Age, and this system is adapted, broadly speaking, to a life of settled habits and unchanging routine, alternating only with occasional outbursts of war or private vengeance.

There can be no doubt that the continually changing environment in which the modern man lives is fatiguing. Moreover, it means that each generation has to think out its own habits and its own expectations with very much less help from the old than was formerly the rule. The young, no doubt, make mistakes; but the old, when they try to think for them, make even greater mistakes. Habits of thought do not change so quickly in the individual as does the mechanical technique of life, so that the habits and opinions of the old seem archaic to the young.

Consider the Russian peasant whose father's ideas were those inherited from the original Byzantine missionaries of the seventh or eighth centuries. Imagine this man confronted with the doctrines of Communism, with Ford tractors, film propaganda, and all the apparatus of modern life. His attitude is likely to be one of bewilderment, either admiring or horrified according to his temperament. In China the gulf covered by an individual who becomes modern is even greater. His father held piously to the doctrines of Confucius, who lived in the sixth century before Christ, while he, if he has had a modern education, considers Communism and American big business the only alternatives worthy of consideration. This sort of thing produces a state of nervous tension tending toward hysteria.

When the rate of progress in the whole world has become as great as it now is in Russia and China, and perhaps even greater, it is to be feared that the whole human race will become hysterical, with the exception of a few stolid individuals too stupid to notice what is happening. This state of affairs is likely to produce and is indeed already tending to produce a world of instability and insanity without landmarks, without unquestioned habits, without settled convictions, but with increasingly passionate devotion to excitement offering destruction. I think it not unlikely that the natural limit to the possible rapidity of human progress will be set by some such collective hysteria.

The only alternative that I can see is that man may grow less intelligent and therefore make fewer inventions. If this should happen, it may be possible to maintain a steady rate of progress not too rapid for the human organism to endure. I have some hope that the educational systems of the world may produce this beneficial result.

23 December 1931

On Snobbery

Of the bad qualities of my own country one of the chief is snobbery. Not that snobbery is confined to England: it is almost more in evidence in the self-governing Dominions and is by no means unknown in America. In the first days of the United States, the leaders of society tried hard to establish hereditary titles in imitation of the British practice but were fortunately defeated by the democratic forces under the leadership of Jefferson. To this day, not a few Americans display a surprising interest in titles. Of this I can speak from experience. Having always held the view that hereditary distinctions are a mistake, I have done all in my power to prevent all mention of such distinctions in my own case. But not infrequently I have encountered a considerable reluctance in this respect, and sometimes hostesses beseech me to allow myself to be introduced by my title.

The reasons for this are not wholly bad. Variety is amusing and picturesque. I derive pleasure myself from visits of Buddhist dignitaries and Sufi literati. I like to meet Italians who have names known to me from Renaissance history. The line between these feelings and those that constitute snobbery is a very narrow one, and yet I cannot feel that there is any harm in them. Insofar as pleasure in titles is of this sort it is innocent.

Snobbery becomes a serious evil when it leads to false standards of value and to tolerance of social inequality. The man who is respected merely for being the son of his father loses one of the normal incentives to useful effort. He is likely to develop views of life which attach undue importance to the accident of birth and to think that by merely existing he does enough to command respect. He believes himself rather better than other men and therefore becomes rather worse. All distinctions not based upon intrinsic merit have this bad effect upon character and on this ground, if on no other, deserve to be abolished.

But the effect upon the man or woman who admires titles

without possessing them is worse because the class concerned is a larger one. Admiration of the kind of merit which is acquired by the exertions of its possessor is useful since it encourages men to do their best. But there is nothing admirable in being the son of one's father, whoever he may have been. Even in America, many people will listen with respect to the opinions of a fool or a charlatan if he happens to be socially distinguished, while a poor man without social culture has to be immensely intelligent in order to make himself felt. All this is foolish and helps to give currency to foolish ideas.

The greatest field for snobbery is the Monarchy, which succeeds in doing more harm than most English people suppose. Few people can bring themselves to treat the opinions of a monarch with no more respect than they would show to those of a common mortal, and yet the education and surroundings of royalty are hardly such as to promote intelligence. In England, while the King has no power to dictate policy, he has the right to have it explained to him by the Prime Minister and to express his opinion of it privately to the Prime Minister. A democratic politician is very likely to be overawed by the unaccustomed pomp and to be led, almost unconsciously, into a deference for royal judgements, which is not likely to be advantageous to the public.

All this trouble arises from the practice of paying deference to a man for reasons which do not imply any superior abilities on his part. This practice is therefore regrettable, and the United States is fortunate in being officially free from it. Socially, it exists in America as elsewhere, but fortunately the socially prominent are not necessarily possessed of much influence upon public affairs. If they were, America might soon become as snob-ridden as Great Britain.

30 December 1931

Whose Admiration Do You Desire?

Many people believe that they live for the approval of their own conscience, and that they are strong enough to ignore what others think of them. There are some few of whom this is true, but they are much fewer than is commonly supposed. Excepting a few heroes, people differ, not as to whether they desire admiration or not, but as to whose admiration they hope to secure.

The average man desires the respect of his colleagues, of his wife and children (if possible), and of his underlings. He hopes that his business associates do not consider him a simple fellow whom anybody could take in. He takes pains not to realise how well his wife knows him. He tries to persuade himself that in a crisis his children would turn to him for advice. The average married woman lives to impress other married women. She tries to persuade them that her husband is richer than theirs and her children more successful. If she is well-to-do, she tries to display better taste than her neighbours in the management and decoration of her house. As they are playing the same game, this requires great skill and much thought.

The desire to impress a wider public arises in either of two opposite ways. It may be too easy to impress one's immediate circle, or it may be too difficult. In either case, a man will seek the admiration, either of the general body of his contemporaries, or of a select body of his successors. Many successful writers, like the Brontë sisters, are acclaimed for their books, though their personal qualities were not such as to impress their neighbours. Anatole France's Pontius Pilate, having incurred the Emperor's displeasure, consoles himself with the thought that 'posterity will do me justice'. Julius Caesar, having always had easy social successes, set himself a harder task and tried to rival Alexander as a historical figure. The eminent men of antiquity and of the

Renaissance lived consciously and avowedly for posthumous fame. An Italian magnate of the sixteenth century, on his death-bed, told the priest that he repented of only one thing, namely, that he had not taken advantage of an opportunity to murder both the Pope and the Emperor at once, which would have secured him a place in history.

The desire for posthumous fame has grown less than it was in those days, because of the growth of newspapers. Contemporary fame can now be so much greater than it could be in former times that it has almost crowded out the wish for the slender trickle of admiration derivable from the readers of history. The fame of a film star at the present day far exceeds that of Alexander or Caesar at the height of his career. Probably more people know the name of Einstein now than have known the name of Archimedes in all the centuries from his day to our own. The effect of all this is that admiration is sought in more ephemeral forms than those formerly desired. Men's work becomes less statuesque, and there is more effort to make it appeal to all and sundry.

Nevertheless, in most prominent men, one form of the desire for posthumous fame lingers, namely the fear of having anything known that will look bad in their biography. Read the life of almost any man who has achieved eminence, and you will find that, at a certain stage, he ceased to live quite spontaneously and began to have an eye on his biographer. This leads to a certain vein of hypocrisy and humbug from which few elderly eminent men are quite free. Admiration is seldom bestowed for what is admirable, and therefore those who seek it successfully seldom deserve it.

December 1931

On National Greatness

What does the greatness of one's country do for the individual? It does something important and not altogether easy to analyse. As a member of a nation which is beginning to lose the great position it has occupied during the last two centuries, I am acutely conscious of the change in individual mentality brought about by the change in political status. And in America, which I have known since 1896, the converse change is taking place, though it is still far from being completely accomplished. Let us try to see what these two opposite changes consist of.

There can be no doubt that national success is a stimulus to individual achievement. When the Athenians had beaten the Persians they built the Parthenon and produced Aeschylus. When the English had defeated the Spaniards they produced Shakespeare. The victories of Louis XIV were associated with the great age of French literature. Instances of this sort of thing could be multiplied indefinitely.

There is a kind of individual productivity which is seldom found except in connection with successful national effort. There are other kinds which have no such connection. Bach, Mozart and Beethoven had no national successes to stimulate their musical genius. Spinoza belonged to an oppressed race and to a nation in process of defeat. What is the difference between greatness which is individual and greatness dependent upon social causes?

The most obvious example of achievement depending on public prosperity is architecture, for the simple reason that architecture is expensive. During the present century America has led the world in architecture because American architects have had opportunities denied to those of other nations. But the architecture, in turn, has reacted on the average man.

The New Yorker, when he talks about the Empire State Building, has a sense of civic pride not always to be derived from his municipal government. The architect's success is, in some degree, the success of every citizen. If he has an argument with a foreigner, one of the causes of his self-confidence will be the fact that the foreigner has no skyscrapers to boast of. The present times have somewhat mitigated this attitude, but that will pass.

The effect of national success is greatest where the young are concerned. Remarkable achievement requires, in the individual, two conditions: first, ability, partly congenital and partly the result of education; second, confidence in his own capacity to accomplish things not possible for the average man. It is this second condition that is influenced by political circumstances.

Some silly person started the notion that true genius is always modest. This is the opposite of the truth; a youth, even if he has capacity, will, if he is modest, be kept under by the mockery of parents and companions – for the pretensions of genius are considered laughable until they are verified.

The best hope for the young is that they should live in an atmosphere where everybody is thought capable of great deeds and where, consequently, their pretensions do not arouse the ridicule that springs from envy. In America, success in business, in the professions, in architecture (which is a business as well as an art) is regarded as a natural and worthy ambition in a young man. Mozart and Beethoven were born into families where success in music was regarded as natural. Such expectations on the part of surrounding adults have an immense influence on youthful ambition and do more than anything else to determine the general direction of national success.

The moral is: Expect of the young the very best of which they are capable, and you will get it. Expect less, and it is only too likely that you will get no more than you expect.

20 January 1932

Is the World Going Mad?

The world at the present day is suffering from two misfortunes: there are people who desire goods which they cannot purchase, and there are people who have goods which they cannot sell. Those who have goods which they cannot sell are adopting various ingenious means of disposing of their surplus. It would be demoralising to wage earners to pay wages for work not done; therefore they continue to produce the goods that they cannot sell but adopt various means of destroying them after they have been produced. Brazil, which suffers from a surplus of coffee, has taken to using it as fuel on the railways and to burning it on large funeral pyres in lonely valleys. There is a glut of rubber, which is unfortunately made worse by the fact that the natives cannot be restrained from tapping the rubber trees. Fortunately rubber trees are subject to a pest, which has hitherto been combated but which is now about to be encouraged. The world's cotton crop has, in the past, been threatened by the boll weevil, but now the boll weevil is welcomed as a friend, since it helps to prevent overproduction of cotton.

The habit of work has become ingrained in the greater part of the human species and not only the habit of work but, what is worse, the habit of looking for ways by which work can be made more productive. Nobody has thought for a moment that it might be a good thing if somebody could enjoy the produce of human labour. Our morality is ascetic, which makes us regard work as a virtue; it follows that production is good and consumption is bad. This ascetic twist has produced a world system in which half the world is poor because it produces too much and the other half because it consumes too little.

What is the cure for this queer insanity? If we could ask the advice of the boll weevil and the rubber pest, they would have a ready answer. The boll weevil would say: 'You have radically misconceived the purpose of cotton; it does not exist to clothe human beings but to supply nourishment to the boll weevil. Human beings', so I am afraid it might continue, 'have in any case not much to be said for them, and it is unworthy of a pleasant substance such as cotton to be condemned to absorb their perspiration. The boll weevil, on the contrary, fights no wars, has no police force, and does not teach the multiplication table to its young. Clearly, therefore, the sum of sentient happiness in the terraqueous globe will be increased if the boll weevil replaces man.' Perhaps we, as human beings, may be allowed enough partiality for our species to reject this argument. But it is not enough merely to reject it, we ought not to be outdistanced in logic by this humble insect. If we are to refute him, we must behave at least as sensibly as he does. He consumes the cotton when he wants it whereas we keep the cotton in one place and the would-be consumers in another; we then complain of bad trade. It seems clear that to improve trade, we must find some way of bringing goods to those who want them. So far, however, the collective wisdom of mankind has not been equal to this effort. People not yet in asylums suggest that the cure for unemployment due to overproduction is to be sought in longer hours. I think it is clear that to start the economic machine again working normally it will be necessary no longer to demand that each operation should at each moment be profitable. There is food rotting in the West of the United States and Canada; there are unemployed populations starving in all the industrial regions throughout the world. If the food were brought to the starving populations, and they were set to work such as would satisfy the wants of Western farmers, the world would be the richer even if no individual capitalist made a profit. The motive of individual profit has apparently broken down, and only organised public effort will restore the economic life of the world.

27 January 1932

Are We Too Passive?

One of the unforeseen and unintended results of the increasing importance of experts in the modern world is that, in a great many departments of life, the ordinary man has become passive where he used to be active. Time was when almost every youth played football; the game was recommended as healthful exercise and a school of manly fortitude as regards small hurts. Nowadays, football is like the theatre: a spectacle provided by specialists for the delectation of the multitude.

It is no longer expected that the players will get any pleasure from their activities; from their point of view, it is not play but work. They are rewarded for their work either by a salary or, if they belong to a university team, by a scholarship in honour of their academic attainments. The pleasure of the game is not an active pleasure on the part of the players but a passive pleasure on the part of the spectators.

A similar change has occurred in a vast number of other directions. Motor cars have destroyed the habit of walking, the radio has killed the art of conversation, preparations in tins and bottles have almost obviated the necessity of cooking. Read the account of Christmas in Pickwick, and you will be amazed by the number of amusements people invented for themselves. Modern people expect their amusements to be provided for them by others.

It is not only in regard to amusements that men have grown passive, but also in regard to all those forms of skill and all those departments of knowledge in which they are not themselves experts. The old-fashioned farmer was weather-wise, whereas the modern man, if he wishes to form an opinion as to what the weather is going to be, reads the official weather forecast. I have sometimes had the impression that he cannot even tell whether it is wet or fine at the moment without the help of his newspaper. Certainly it is from his newspaper that he derives his opinions on politics and the state of the world and the need of a return to the rugged virtues of a former age. On most matters he does not trouble to have opinions at all, since he is convinced that they can safely be left to those whose special study or experience entitles them to speak with authority.

In some directions this respect for authority is good, while in others it is harmful and even ludicrous. The mother who has acquired a taste for child psychology is continually having to run from her child to her textbook and back again, to solve problems of which more instinctive mothers were not even aware.

The infant drops his toy and howls to have it picked up. If it is picked up he acquires a power-complex, if it is left lying on the floor he acquires a rage-complex. The book says something very good on this point and the mother turns the pages frantically to find the passage. By the time she has found it the child is thinking of something else. But after a sufficient number of such experiences, he acquires a low opinion of mothers.

To avoid too much passivity is an educational problem. It demands, in play, the absence of elaborate apparatus and no undue respect for exceptional skill; in work, encouragement of active investigation rather than mere listening to knowledge imparted by means of lectures. Unfortunately the authorities like passivity because it is convenient.

3 February 1932

Why We Enjoy Mishaps

It is a curious fact that nine people out of ten become happier when faced with some small misfortune. On my first visit to America, thirty-five years ago, a train in which I was travelling became stuck in a snowdrift so that we did not arrive in New York until a great many hours after all the food on the train had been eaten up. I was beginning to expect that the passengers would draw lots as to who should be eaten, but, far from that, everybody was in the best of spirits. People who would have hated each other in ordinary circumstances found each other quite agreeable, and everybody reached an obviously exceptional level of happiness.

I have observed the same thing in a really bad London fog. An ordinary fog is a mere nuisance, but a fog so bad that you cannot see your own feet brings consolation even to the most melancholic. People begin to speak to complete strangers – a thing which in London is not much done. They recall the far worse fogs that they remember in their youth; they tell of friends who got lost at Hyde Park Corner and were only found again by accidentally running into a policeman in quite another part of the town.

Everybody laughs, everybody is jolly – until the fog clears, when they again become sober, grave and responsible citizens.

Unfortunately this mood, which is appropriate enough for small mishaps that cannot be prevented, is apt to extend itself to large misfortunes that could have been avoided. I have never been in a shipwreck, an eruption or a serious earthquake, and I am prepared to believe that these experiences are not wholly pleasant. But I do remember the beginning of the Great War, and everybody's mood then was almost exactly what it is in a bad fog – one of hilarious and excited friendliness. In the first days there were very few who were saddened by the prospect of horrors to come. Light-hearted confidence was the order of the day in all the countries concerned.

There are two reasons for this curious excess of happiness in circumstances where the opposite would seem more natural. The first is love of excitement. Most of us go about the world oppressed by boredom; if an elephant falls into our coal cellar or a tree crashes through our plate-glass windows and smashes our best drawing-room furniture, the incident is, of course, in itself regrettable, but the mere fact that it is unusual redeems it. We have something to tell our neighbours about and may hope to be a centre of interest for the next twenty-four hours. Excitement in itself is agreeable, though of course it would be pleasanter if the excitement had a pleasant source, such as inheriting a fortune from a millionaire uncle.

In the cases of the snowdrift, the fog and the war, there was, however, another element – namely, the fact that everybody was feeling alike. As a rule, each of us is occupied with his own concerns; other people may hinder us, or bore us, or fail altogether to attract our notice. But there are occasions on which a common emotion actuates a whole crowd. When this happens, even if the emotion in itself is not pleasant, the fact that it is shared gives a peculiar happiness not obtainable in any other way.

If we could all be habitually in a state of collective emotion, we should all be always happy, always co-operative and always free from boredom. Perhaps the government psychologists of the future will obtain this result. Public holidays will begin with a huge sky-writing, saying: 'The Martians are attempting to invade you. Every man, woman, and child can do his, her, or its bit.' Toward evening it would be announced that the attack had been repulsed. In this way everybody would be sure of a happy holiday. But these are among the triumphs of science for which the world is not yet ripe.

10 February 1932

Does Education Do Harm?

I happened to be reading lately biographies of a number of men who achieved great eminence during the nineteenth century. It is a remarkable fact that very few of them had much of what is conventionally called education. Jay Gould had only one year's schooling; Commodore Vanderbilt apparently even less. It is said by those who know that 'he was totally without education, and could write hardly half a dozen lines without outraging the spelling-book'.[5] Carnegie never went to school after he was twelve; the list could be lengthened indefinitely. I think it will be found on examination that almost all the men who made the age in which we live, so far as business organisation is concerned, were men unencumbered by the heritage of culture which it is supposed to be the business of the universities to transmit. Some of them are conscious of the benefits they have derived from struggle in youth. Mr John D. Rockefeller states in his reminiscences that he counts it among his blessings to have been brought up in a family of modest means.[6] Nevertheless he has taken pains to prevent his own children from enjoying this blessing.

What applies to wealth applies also to education. Many men who have achieved eminence believe, probably rightly, that they have profited by the lack of formal education; yet not one of them would abstain from giving a first-class education to his son. Carnegie, for example, did his utmost to inflict this doubtful blessing upon vast numbers of poor young men in Scotland. It would seem, therefore, that whatever we may think about education in our speculative moments, we all of us, as practical men, regard its value as unquestionable.

I wonder whether we are right in this. I have no doubt that we should be right if education were what it ought to be, but only too often the educator kills initiative in his pupils by teaching them that it is more important to be right than to be original and that to be right is to agree with the teacher. Education, moreover, teaches people that the way to find out things is to look them up in books, not to observe them in the actual world. I can remember when I was a child being made to read an account of the squirrel by the famous naturalist Buffon in which he asserted that the squirrel hardly ever descends to the ground. I knew a great deal about squirrels through observation and was aware that on this point the great man was talking nonsense. My teacher, however, knew nothing about squirrels, and I therefore found it imprudent to pit my knowledge against Buffon's romance. The teacher almost invariably tends to believe what is in books because they are convenient and can be brought into the schoolroom. The habits of the hippopotamus, for example, cannot well be studied from the life by a class in school. Galileo used to drop weights from the Leaning Tower of Pisa to see how they fell; this was considered by his colleagues to be a waste of his students' time since they ought to have been sitting at their desks finding out how bodies fall from the pages of Aristotle and not from observation.

University students are allowed nowadays to know how bodies fall, but they are not allowed to know how men rise. I have read publications by the university presses of famous American universities which turn American captains of industry into models of Sunday School propriety, apparently in order to instil into the youth of America the belief that if they do as they are told by their professors they may all become plutocrats. It is considered the business of education in all countries to substitute edification for the giving of knowledge and to instil false beliefs with the mistaken notion that only by lies can the young be led to become virtuous. All this springs, to my mind, from a false conception of virtue, the 'fugitive and cloistered virtue' which Milton denounced.[7] Real virtue is robust and in contact with facts, not with pretty-pretty fancies. We have chosen to hedge round the profession of teaching with such restrictions that, in the main, those who choose this profession are men and women who are afraid of reality, and we have done this because, while many of us recognise that contact with reality has been good for us, few of us have the courage to believe that it is good for our children. This is the fundamental reason why education, as it exists, is so unsatisfactory.

17 February 1932

Are Men of Science Scientific?

Ordinary men and women are, for the most part, aware that there are many matters as to which their own personal judgement is not wholly trustworthy. They look about the world anxiously for founts of wisdom, and by placing their trust in them they arrive at a comfortable certainty. Savages trusted the medicine man, who by slow stages developed into the priest. The priest is being succeeded by the physician, the physician by the man of science. The man of science in general (though there are honourable exceptions) is nothing loath to take up the position which the public offers him. He is willing to make pronouncements about the laziness of the wage-earning classes, the superiority of the Nordic races, the eugenic superiority of the rich, and any other topics that may at the moment be of political interest.

For the genuine man of science I have the highest possible respect. He is the one force in the modern world at once genuinely constructive and profoundly revolutionary. When the man of science is dealing with technical matters that do not touch upon the prejudices which he shares with the average man, he is more likely to be right than anyone else. But unfortunately very few men of science are able to retain their impartiality when they come to matters about which they feel strongly. For example, every male student of the human brain is persuaded in advance that men's brains are better than women's. When it was found that the average weight of a man's brain is greater than that of a woman's, this was held as proof of his superior intellectuality. When it was pointed out that an elephant's brain is even heavier, the eminent scientists scratched their heads since they could not admit that their wits were elephantine. Somebody suggested that the important thing is the proportion of the weight of the brain to the weight of the body. But this had a disastrous result: it seemed to show that women were, on the whole, cleverer than men. This would never do. So they said that it was not mere brute weight that mattered but delicacy of organisation. As this was still a matter conjecture, it could be assumed to be better in men than in women.

There is a great deal of pseudo-scientific nonsense talked about heredity. Writers of eugenics are, with few exceptions, Nordics belonging to the professional classes. It follows that the Nordics are the best race and the professional classes the best stock within that race. For these propositions, which are fundamental in the speculation of eugenists, the evidence offered is of a very flimsy kind. The mountaineers of the Alleghenies, who are racially among the purest of the inhabitants of the United States, do not come out so well by the intelligence tests as do the Jews. This shows, we are told, that there is something inadequate about the intelligence tests and that we must take account also of moral qualities. But no evidence is offered that poor whites surpass the Jews in moral qualities.

The study of heredity was revolutionised by a monk named Mendel, who spent his time growing peas. It has become much more difficult than used to be supposed to know what ought to be done if a defect which can be inherited is to be eliminated. Some people's fingers have only two joints instead of three; it seems that the methods that have been proposed for dealing with the feeble-minded would be quite successful in eliminating these people with abnormal fingers but would take thousands of years to eliminate the feeble-minded. This is because the kind of inheritance in the two cases is different. But the alliance between politicians and pseudo-scientists is so strong that it will take a long time before such facts become commonly known. The general public cannot tell which among scientists is to be trusted and will therefore be wise to be very sceptical whenever they hear a man of science giving a confident opinion about a matter on which he has strong prejudices. Men of science are not supermen and are as liable to error as the rest of us.

24 February 1932

Flight from Reality

Why do people read? The answer, as regards the great majority, is: 'They don't.' The majority of mankind read nothing at all; of the remainder, the majority read only the picture papers. Of those who read something more than picture papers, the majority never gets as far as books. All the readers of books – grave and gay, profound and superficial, scientific, literary or lurid – all put together are a very small fraction of the population. Nevertheless they differ among themselves in all sorts of ways. There are those who read in order to acquire information; they are generally very young. There are those who read in order to acquire confirmation of their prejudices; these people are what is called mature. But the great bulk of readers are seeking neither knowledge nor support for their own opinions, but an escape from reality into the world of imagination.

This escape takes all sorts of forms. The crudest kind is that supplied by many novelettes and films, where an obscure young man or woman achieves conspicuous success or a rich marriage. At a slightly higher level come those who seek escape in history and in imagining the glories of past ages. A still further stage is reached in such subjects as astronomy. The success of such books as those of Jeans and Eddington is partly due to the fact that the stars seem to have a very quiet life; they are not troubled by the tax collector, or by the illnesses of their children, or by business depression. If you can once identify yourself in imagination with a star or a nebula, you will find it wonderfully soothing.

But people do not only desire to be soothed, they desire also to be excited. For my part, it is this latter desire that dictates most of my reading. I am in the habit of saying that I never read the sort of books that I write. If I could write the sort of books that I read, I would do so; but this talent has been denied me. My favourite reading consists of detective stories. If I could write detective stories, I should have no doubt that I had contributed to human happiness, which, as things are, remains open to question.

Detective stories, poetry, and astronomy, all represent different forms of the escape from what is called 'reality'. We are told by psychoanalysis that the desire to escape from reality is a very bad thing, but to my mind they exaggerate and fail to make some necessary distinctions. The desire to escape from reality becomes a bad thing when it produces delusions or causes a man to neglect his business. A man may become so poor and be so harassed by his creditors that he finds relief in believing himself to be president of the Bank of France. This form of escape from reality is to be deplored. A young woman may become so absorbed in romantic tales of the King Cophetua type that she neglects her work and finally loses her job. This also is to be deplored. But there are other forms of escape from reality which are wholly desirable. Mozart used to compose music in order to forget his duns and his debts by escaping into a world of phantasy. If he had followed the advice of eminent psychoanalysts, he would instead have drawn up a careful balance sheet of receipts and expenditures and set to work to devise economies by which the two could be made to balance. If he had done this, he would have lost his income, and we should have lost his music. Escape from reality, as this instance shows, is not undesirable when it is into a world of imagination recognised as such and used as a means of making reality itself more tolerable.

I believe that without this motive of escape from reality, almost all the most delightful things in the world would have failed to be produced. I am therefore of the opinion that those whose reading is dictated by this motive – the desire to escape – are not on that account to be condemned.

2 March 1932

Illegal?

Shortly after the war, when Austria was in a very bad way, an Austrian farmer hanged himself from the branch of a tree. A neighbour saw him and cut him down before life was extinct. The farmer brought an action against the neighbour on the ground that the neighbour had inflicted a further dose of life on him, which constituted a tort, in view of the fact that life in Austria at that time was an evil. The court appeared to agree with the farmer, though it acquitted the neighbour on some technicality.

In England and in large parts of America the view taken of attempted suicide is different: it is held that suicide is murder and that attempted suicide is attempted murder. When a man finds life so painful that he tries to kill himself he is given a dose of prison to teach him to find life more pleasant.

This seems to me doubly irrational. In the first place, attempted suicide ought not to be considered a crime; in the second place, imprisonment is not likely in this case to prove a deterrent.

To say that it is as bad to kill yourself as to kill someone else seems to me absurd. If I take someone else's watch and throw it into the sea, I'm a criminal, but if I throw my own watch into the sea, I am at worst foolish, and if the watch is worthless, I may even be quite sensible. What applies to my watch applies also to my life. When I take another man's life I am taking what does not belong to me, but the question of taking my own life is clearly one that concerns me more than it does any one else.

It may be said that I ought not to take my life because it is capable of being useful to others. In many cases this is sound as a moral argument, but it is not wise to make the law as exacting as private ethics. One might say the same thing of property: it may be immoral to throw away even a worthless watch when one considers how much pleasure it might give to some small boy, but that would scarcely be an adequate ground for putting a man in prison if he throws away his own watch after it has ceased to go. It may be, in like manner, that every man could put the remaining years of his life to some good use. But there are many men who do not see any way of doing so, and not a few whose death would be no great loss to the community. In any case, a man's life, like his property, ought to be legally his, and if he chooses to throw it away he should be allowed to do so.

From the deterrent point of view, the punishment of attempted suicide is futile. The man who attempts suicide expects to succeed and therefore to escape punishment; while the man who has failed and been punished is not likely to find life more agreeable after a period in prison.

The subject of suicide is apt to be considered not on its merits but in relation to what is called the sacredness of human life. I find, however, that it is illegal to take this phrase seriously, since those who do so are compelled to condemn war. So long as war remains part of our institutions it is mere hypocrisy to invoke the sacredness of human life against those unfortunates whose misery leads them to attempt suicide.

9 March 1932

On Optimism

Once upon a time there was a derelict ship which drifted into the empty parts of the southern ocean and began to run out of provisions. Most of the crew took each day as it came, but there were two exceptions: one was a professional pessimist, the other was a professional optimist. The professional pessimist pointed out continually how low the stock of food was becoming and how seldom ships were encountered in such latitudes. He advised his comrades to meditate on their latter end and to prepare for death with fortitude. One day they turned on him and advised him to prepare for death with fortitude himself during the five minutes of life that they were prepared to leave him. When he had been heaved overboard, they gave a sigh of relief.

But in this they were mistaken. So long as the pessimist lived, the rest of the crew had been grateful to the optimist, but now they began to find him just as trying as they had previously found his opponent. Every morning he came on deck, rubbing his hands and smiling, pointing out how long the human frame can subsist on half a biscuit, and making elaborate calculations to show that on that day they would probably meet a ship. In the end they threw him overboard also and got on with the job.

The moral of this story is that believers in every kind of 'ism' ought to hang together, however opposite their nostrums may be. They differ from ordinary people by the fact that they have a nostrum. One man's nostrum is only endurable to the ordinary person when it is counterbalanced by another man's nostrum. If the believers in any one 'ism' could convert the believers in all other 'isms' to their way of thinking, the general run of mankind would find them so boring that they would soon exterminate them. This applies to the believers in optimism no less than to the believers in pessimism. The pessimism of our age is generally explained as being due to the bad state of the world, but I believe it is quite as much due to the boredom which we all endured in youth through the optimism of the Victorians.

The fact is that optimism is pleasant so long as it is credible, but when it is not, it is intensely irritating. Especially irritating is the optimism about our own troubles which is displayed by those who do not have to share them. Optimism about other people's troubles is a very risky business unless it goes with quite concrete proposals as to how to make the troubles disappear or grow less. A medical man has a right to be optimistic about your illness if he can prescribe a treatment which will cure it, but a friend who merely says, 'Oh, I expect you will soon feel better,' is exasperating. Most of the people who have talked optimistically throughout the last two years about the bad times have been in the position of the cheerful friend rather than of the medical adviser, and I doubt whether their cheerfulness has added much to the happiness of those who were starving.

In every kind of trouble what is wanted is not emotional cheerfulness but constructive thinking. This fact is gradually being borne in upon the world by the world-wide depression, and in this I perceive the only basis for optimism that our present troubles afford. These troubles can be cured by constructive thinking, not by ballyhoo.

16 March 1932

As Others See Us

There are some who maintain that the knowledge which a man has of himself is more to be trusted than any knowledge which an outsider can obtain concerning him. They say that true comprehension of any matter requires that it should be viewed from within. Those who say this are partly philosophers and partly kindly moralists, urging us not to think ill of our neighbours until we have seen matters from their point of view. On the other hand, practical men of the world always trust the outside judgement more than that from inside. What are we to think in this disagreement?

I think the answer depends upon whether you are interested in what a man feels or in what he does. If you want to understand what a man feels, you must learn to put yourself inside his skin and to see the world from his point of view. But if you want to know what he would do, you will find it wiser to regard him quite externally, as an astronomer regards the moon or the planet Jupiter. The difference between the two points of view comes out most clearly where the acts of nations are concerned.

Take, for example, the behaviour of the British in India. To most English people it seems that Anglo-Indians have been struggling heroically to spread the light of civilisation in the face of obscurantism, intolerance and surperstition. To almost everybody who is not British, the British appear in India as brutal tyrants, enjoying power and extracting tribute. If you wish to know how an Anglo-Indian feels, you must adopt the British point of view; whereas if you want to know what he does, you must adopt the point of view of the rest of the world. The same thing may be said of the doings of Americans in Haiti and Central America, and of imperialist doings generally.

But if the view from outside is to lead to the truth, it must be rather more dispassionate than is usually the case when one nation is passing judgement upon another. There are those who say that love is the key to understanding, but if scientific understanding is meant, I do not think they are right. It would, however, be even more unscientific to regard hatred as the key to understanding.

Every emotion, whether friendly or unfriendly, distorts judgement. If astronomers had regarded the moon either as a deity or as a devil, it would have taken them much longer to construct an adequate theory of the moon's motions. Where human beings are concerned there is, however, a difficulty. We do not, as a rule, take a very great interest in the doings of other people unless we either love or hate them. If we do not take an interest in them, we do not take the trouble to get information about them; while if we either love or hate them, the information which we shall obtain is likely to be misinformation. This applies in particular to one nation's knowledge of another nation.

I imagine that most Americans view Latvia, for example, without either love or hate, and the consequence is that they know nothing about Latvia. If they love or hate a country their newspapers will supply them with favourable or unfavourable information, as the case may be, and their prejudices will gradually come to be confirmed by a mass of what appears to be knowledge.

We touch here upon one of the difficulties of democracy. After people leave school their knowledge of foreign countries, such as it is, is derived from the newspapers, and they will not buy a newspaper unless it flatters their prejudices. Consequently, the only knowledge they obtain is such as to confirm their preconceptions and passions.

This is one of the great difficulties in the way of a sane conduct of international affairs, and I do not see how it is to be dealt with within the limits of nationalist democracy.

23 March 1932

Taking Long Views

There are those who say that they take no interest in what happens to the world after they are dead. For my part, this is not the way I feel. I like to think that present actions may bear fruit in the future, even if I shall not personally take part in that future. I like to think that civilisation will continue to improve, and the opposite thought when it comes, as it sometimes will, is depressing. In these days, when the immediate outlook is somewhat gloomy, the thought of a more distant future is often cheering.

In the nineteenth century men took progress for granted, and, especially after people had begun to believe in evolution, it was thought to be a law of nature that the future must be better than the past. In this cheerful frame of mind people did not trouble to think of distant ages. Even utopias were expected to be realised in a century or two. Since 1914 this optimism has grown less sure of itself, and during the present depression it has yielded to pessimism in the minds of very many.

Pessimism, however, is only called for as regards the next hundred years or so. After that it is quite likely that mankind may enter upon an era of happiness, peace and prosperity. Long views are therefore beginning to be the fashion among those who wish to encourage optimism. The astronomers tell us that the human race is likely to persist for another billion years or so, which leaves the optimists plenty of time. For my part I derive real encouragement from these vast vistas. I read a book recently called *Last and First Men* by Stapledon, which traces the future of mankind through biological eons from the earth to Venus and from Venus to Neptune.[8] I liked in this book the sense of indomitable purpose, at first unconscious, often temporarily defeated, but never permanently baffled – a purpose towards knowledge, towards mastery, towards collective human self direction, and towards fullness of life. I agree with the author of this book in thinking that this purpose, having come into the world with that measure of intelligence with which mankind at present combines it, will not easily be defeated and may survive many cataclysms, both social and physical.

This belief, in those who feel it strongly, is capable of inspiring courage and consistency as regards both public and private affairs. It is, to my mind, one which ought to be fostered in schools. At present in most countries history is taught from a national standpoint, but nations grow and decay, so that purely national hopes have necessarily a chronological limit, however vague. Moreover, those elements of national greatness which are most emphasised in the teaching of history are such things as conquest and dominion, which are not contributions to the collective glory of mankind. To make this collective glory visible there should be teaching of the pre-human geological record of the early struggles of modern man and of the history of civilisation as a whole. In this record of the past a general movement is discernible, and the student imperceptibly acquires the desire to continue the same upward movement into the future. The glory of individual men may consist in victory over their fellow men, but the glory of man consists in intelligent collective purpose and collective mastery over the environment as well as over what is archaic in his own nature. I believe that in the not very distant future the adversity caused by the pursuit of merely national aims on the part of separate national groups will lead mankind to a more vivid realisation than exists at present of these collective purposes which justify man's existence in the universe.

30 March 1932

On Mental Differences Between Boys and Girls

The feminists of a generation ago were inclined to minimise the inevitable differences between men and women and to ascribe the differences which are observed to education rather than to nature. They thought that a little feminine tyranny would make men as virtuous as women and a little masculine training would make women as intelligent as men. With these hopes they proceeded to a heroic campaign for the emancipation of women. Their hopes, however, have not been realised. Some assimilation there has been: there is no longer a double standard, but this result has been achieved, so far as the young are concerned, mainly by approximating the standard for women to that for men, not by the opposite process for which the pioneer women hoped. As regards intelligence, the attempts to ignore native differences are beginning to seem a mistake. A great deal of the scholastic education of men is worthless, and it is a pity to inflict it on women. The most important part of men's education is the most masculine, namely, that concerned with science and machinery, and it is this part especially which almost always fails to arouse feminine interest.

I have had in recent years opportunity to observe a group of very young boys and girls brought up in a careful atmosphere of sex equality where the education offered to the two sexes is precisely the same. I have found that the more freedom boys and girls have, the more masculine and feminine they respectively become. Boys spend all their leisure talking about aeroplanes and motor cars and electricity, and such topics. Girls like dolls, constructing play houses, looking after pet animals, sewing, arts and crafts, and so on. If their wider intellectual interests are to be aroused, it must be through biological rather than physical sciences. I think this difference between boys and girls is innate and nearly universal.

It would be foolish to draw the inference that female intelligence is inferior to that of the male. Men have set a standard of intelligence and have instinctively set it to suit themselves; they have created a mechanical civilisation which largely ignores human values. Women left to themselves would, I believe, never have invented machines. But if they had been able freely to contribute to the sum total of civilisation, they would not have forgotten to preserve what is valuable in human life and would not have been led astray, as men have been, by a blind worship of mechanical ingenuity.

The older feminists were wrong, I think, in supposing men and women to be alike by nature and differing only by training, but they were right in thinking that men and women should be equals and have an equal contribution to make to civilisation. The contribution which women's nature would enable them to make, they have not yet been able to make, because they have not been free. They have been exposed to an education designed for men, and they have been debarred by prudery from the kind of education which would have most developed their faculties. This state of affairs, however, is rapidly improving, and I think we may hope that before many decades have passed women will be in a position to be no longer either restrictive or imitative but genuinely creative in important ways for which their faculties are more adapted than those of men.

6 April 1932

On the Fierceness of Vegetarians

I do not know whether any of my readers have ever contemplated starting a crank school; if they have I strongly urge them to abandon the idea at once. The crank schoolmaster is considered fair game by all the other cranks throughout the world, who all express astonishment when they discover that he does not believe in their particular nostrum. There are those who think that Mexican Indian medicine men are repositories of ancient Egyptian wisdom; there are those who are convinced that the Great Pyramid foretells the course of the world's history from the date of its construction to the year 1932; there are those who believe that the English are the Ten Lost Tribes; there are those who consider themselves to be reincarnations of Julius Ceasar. From all these I have personally suffered.

More troublesome than any of these is the vegetarian. There is a popular notion that vegetarians are mild and gentle folk who would not hurt a fly. Perhaps they would not hurt a fly. As to this, I cannot speak, but their charity towards flies certainly does not extend to human beings. Perhaps the most powerful argument in favour of a vegetarian diet is the vigour and pugnacity which it gives to those who practise it.

I had a letter recently from a lady who stated that she had travelled many thousand miles in order to place her daughter in my 'most wonderful school', as she was pleased to call it. I appointed a day for her to see the institution and prepared to welcome her with appropriate enthusiasm. Unfortunately her eye was caught by the menu giving the children's diet, which she read and commented upon. 'Cereals. Ah yes, very good. Bananas. Yes, admirable. But what is this? Bacon! Am I to understand that you, who wish to create a new world, encourage the innocent children to consume the flesh of their fellow creatures?' She could hardly believe her eyes and proceeded at once to give me a masterly synopsis of the arguments in favour of vegetarianism. I suggested mildly that the subject of diet was one to which some attention had been given after consultation of the best medical authorities and that my opinion was not likely to be changed by a few minutes of conversation, however many thousands of miles the lady might have travelled. She thereupon said, 'Ah, but this is a great disappointment to me. Surely you would not wish to see me weep?' Even this argument did not seem to prove conclusively that meat is bad for children. Finally she offered to become my cook, at no wages, and to halve my food bills. At this point I discovered a pressing engagement elsewhere since it seemed to me that there was no hope except in flight.

This experience is by no means unique. Everybody knows how Mrs Patrick Campbell, after being rehearsed by Bernard Shaw, exclaimed: 'If he should ever eat a beefsteak, God help us.' She evidently had little experience of those who live upon a vegetable diet. Otherwise she would have known that a beefsteak would constitute her best hope. This is not a new phenomenon in the world's history. Abel, as we know, was a meat eater, but Cain agreed with Mr Bernard Shaw on the subject of diet.

13 April 1932

Furniture and the Ego

Most normal human beings experience the need for self-expression, some in a greater degree, some in a less. The means by which they seek to achieve this end vary enormously. Those who enjoy some one thoroughly satisfactory form are often content to seek no other. Great opera singers wander from city to city, living in hotel suites, associating with hosts of strangers, and dispensing almost wholly with everything intimate in their material surroundings; they are able to endure this life because their ego finds complete expression in their art. In a lesser degree the same thing will be found true of most of those who have some exceptional artistic or literary talent.

But most people, and especially most women, desire to externalise their ego in material surroundings which they themselves have assembled or chosen. Many girls when they get married derive quite as much pleasure from their house as from their husband. The bare core of personality, as it exists in our own thoughts and feelings, is too tenuous and invisible to be wholly satisfying, so that most of us wish to see in the outer world some reflection of our inner being. We achieve this in varying degrees. The man whose name is advertised on every hoarding perhaps achieves it most, but such a depth of bliss is not for ordinary mortals. The typical housewife seeks self-expression in curtains and carpets, tables and chairs, dinner service and coffee cups. There are some to whom the process of furnishing is intimate and personal, the collection of a work of art which has individual beauty, specially appropriate to the temperament of its creator. There are others, however – and in the modern world they are the large majority – whose ego is more shy and timid. Their highest aspiration is to be thought exactly like their neighbours, and in their furniture they seek correctness rather than the expression of their own taste. According to their means, they buy complete sets from Grand Rapids,[9] or furnish exquisite period suites that could be transferred bodily to a museum. The trade of the interior decorator thrives on this timidity. Tolstoy describes somewhere a newly married couple who are giving their first evening party; when it is over, they congratulate each other on the fact that it has been exactly like anyone else's evening party. Those to whom this is the highest ambition evidently fear contempt more than they hope for admiration, and in so far as they do hope for admiration they hope to secure it by successful imitation rather than by any genuine intrinsic quality. They may acquire taste, which can be learnt by those who take the necessary trouble, but they cannot acquire spontaneous enjoyment of the things that appear beautiful to them, whatever others may think of them.

Fear of our neighbours is one of our most deep-seated emotions and is the enemy of all achievement, even in so comparatively simple a matter as furnishing a sitting room. We force this upon each other by our unfriendly censoriousness, by means of which we make each other dull and deprive ourselves of the pleasures to be derived from the spectacle of vigorous individuality expressing itself freely. Thus the source of ugly furniture is the same as the source of war and religious persecution, and of all the major evils of human life.

20 April 1932

Why Are We Discontented?

It seems to be generally accepted that quiet contentment is very rare in the present age. It is apt to be assumed that in other ages it was commoner, though this is to my mind very doubtful. If an indictment is to be framed against our time it must not be on the ground that people are less contented than they were but rather on the ground that in spite of improved conditions they have not grown more contented.

We have realised what were formerly supposed to be the conditions for a happy life more than has happened in any earlier age. Even in the present bad times there are more comforts and luxuries than there ever were before. Especially there are more amusements and fewer occasions for boredom. Nevertheless, it is doubtful whether any but the poorest sections of society are appreciably happier than they were in former times.

Certainly modern literature is, as a rule, far from optimistic. When a man like Priestley tries to re-create the jollity of Pickwick, his work is felt to be artificial and an anachronism.

It is customary to attribute modern pessimism to the decay of faith and the difficulty of finding some continuous and fruitful purpose in life. I doubt, however, whether this is a correct analysis, or, at any rate, whether it goes to the root of the matter. I believe the lack of zest and of fruitful purpose itself has physiological causes. A man in a really good physical condition finds something to believe in, whereas a man whose digestion or glands are out of order is a prey to all the gloomy forms of doubt and despair.

I believe that if our pessimists were subjected to a rigorous regimen of physical exercise, simple but wholesome diet and long hours of sleep, they would begin to find all sorts of things worth doing and would feel hopeful as to the possibility of doing some of these things themselves. Any man who contemplates writing a book or engaging in any forms of preaching or propaganda should be obliged to do an hour's digging or other outdoor manual work before breakfast. By that time breakfast would be such a delight that throughout the rest of the day he would be incapable of thinking that all is vanity.

Those who resisted this regimen and still remained pessimistic should be subjected to something more severe: they should be allowed only an apple and a glass of milk for their breakfast and should be compelled to do outdoor physical exercise until midday. After the midday meal most of them would fall asleep, but the few who remained awake might write books worth reading.

The body has natural rhythms, diurnal and annual, which it acquired during the long ages when men possessed few artificial means of escaping from the rigours of nature. We have emancipated our daily lives from these rigours; our rooms are brightly lit by night and adequately warmed in frosty weather. Those of us whose work is not manual are apt to have far less physical exercise than the health of the body demands; our diet also tends to be rich without being nourishing.

Such homely reasons as these have, I believe, much more to do with the discontent of moderns than has any form of cosmic despair or decay of faith. If I am right, the cure for modern despair is a matter for the physician, not for the philosopher.

I, alas, am a philosopher, not a physician.

27 April 1932

On Locomotion

One of the things that the modern man considers essential to happiness is frequent and rapid change of position relative to terrestrial objects.

The earth's rotation causes the inhabitants of New York to move through about sixteen thousand miles a day; the earth's revolution round the sun takes them on a journey of about three hundred million miles every year; the sun's proper motion causes them to approach the constellation Hercules by several miles in every second. But all this fails to content them. It is not enough to move relatively to the fixed stars; they must move also relatively to Broadway.

In this respect men have changed and are still changing. In Chaucer's day, when two Cambridge undergraduates wished to go to Trumpington, which is between two and three miles from Cambridge, the college authorities considered it necessary that they should spend the night there, as no one could be expected to go and come in one day. Jane Austen's characters regard a young man as very frivolous because he goes to London for the day from Leatherhead, a distance of some fifteen miles.

Nowadays English people fly to Baghdad for the Easter holidays. Soon there will be weekend excursions over the North Pole and afternoon trips across the Sahara.

This increased mobility has produced a great change in the mentality of educated people – more perhaps in Europe than in America, because European travel quickly takes the traveller across frontiers and into different civilisations, while the three thousand miles from New York to Los Angeles produce less change in this respect than the twenty-one miles from Dover to Calais.

It is true that a very complete change is obtainable by crossing the border into Mexico, but it does not occur to the citizens of the United States to regard Mexican civilisation as one from which there is anything to be learned.

In Europe there is no such obvious superiority of one country to another. It might therefore be expected that travel would have the effect of broadening men's outlook, enlarging their sympathies, and increasing their knowledge of mankind. This effect is produced in those who travel in order to do some work which brings them into important relations with the inhabitants of the foreign countries in which they find themselves, but not in those who travel merely in order to travel.

Such people, if they are rich, stay at cosmopolitan hotels which are exactly alike in all the countries of the world and associate with such of their fellow-travellers as they already know at home. If they are poor, they usually travel in large gangs, with a manager who saves them from the necessity of even business contacts with the natives. They come home having experienced nothing except picture-postcards and the railway system.

The habit of constant movement is destroying some things which had considerable value. The practice of reading for pleasure is dying out, especially as regards books that are not quite new. Knowledge of the seasons, and the intimate love of places in their detail that comes of remaining immovable throughout the year, are now almost confined to agricultural labourers. This has caused the poetry of the past, and the ways of feeling from which it sprang, to go dead.

Many valuable emotions, and much important thinking, can only grow up as the result of long periods of quiet. These elements in the emotional and philosophical outlook of the past are now decaying.

On the other hand, the cruelty and madness which in former ages were generated by boredom and unendurable monotony are also growing less. Perhaps therefore there is gain on the balance. However that may be, the mental change is certainly profound, and still only half completed.

11 May 1932

Of Co-operation

In these days, under the influence of democracy, the virtue of co-operation has taken the place formerly held by obedience. The old-fashioned schoolmaster would say of a boy that he was disobedient; the modern schoolmistress says of an infant that he is non-co-operative. It means the same thing: the child, in either case, fails to do what the teacher wishes, but in the first case the teacher acts as the government and in the second as the representative of the People, i.e. of the other children. The result of the new language, as of the old, is to encourage docility, suggestibility, herd-instinct and conventionality, thereby necessarily discouraging originality, initiative and unusual intelligence. Adults who achieve anything of value have seldom been 'co-operative' children. As a rule, they have liked solitude: they have tried to slink into a corner with a book and have been happiest when they could escape the notice of their barbarian contemporaries. Almost all men who have been distinguished as artists, writers or men of science have in boyhood been objects of derision and contempt to their schoolfellows; and only too often the teachers have sided with the herd, because it annoyed them that a boy should be odd.

It ought to be part of the training of all teachers to be taught to recognise the marks of unusual intelligence in children and to restrain the irritation caused in themselves by anything so unusual. Until this is done, a large proportion of the best talent in America will be persecuted out of existence before the age of fifteen. Co-operativeness, as an ideal, is defective: it is right to live with reference to the community and not for oneself alone, but living for the community does not mean doing what it does. Suppose you are in a theatre which catches fire, and there is a stampede: the person who has learnt no higher morality than what is called 'co-operation' will join in the stampede since he will possess no inner force that would enable him to stand up against the herd. The psychology of a nation embarking on a war is at all points identical.

I do not wish, however, to push the doctrine of individual initiative too far. Godwin,[10] who became Shelley's father-in-law because Shelley so much admired him, asserted that 'everything that is usually understood by the term "co-operation" is in some degree an evil'. He admits that, at present, 'to pull down a tree, to cut a canal, to navigate a vessel requires the labour of many', but he looks forward to the time when machinery will be so perfected that one man unaided will be able to do any of these things. He thinks also that hereafter there will be no orchestras. 'Shall we have concerts of music?' he says. 'The miserable state of mechanism of the majority of the performers is so conspicuous as to be even at this day a topic of mortification and ridicule. Will it not be practicable hereafter for one man to perform the whole?' He goes on to suggest that the solitary performer will insist on playing his own productions and refuse to be the slave of composers dead and gone.

All this is, of course, ridiculous, and for my part I find it salutary to see my own opinions thus caricatured. I remain none the less convinced that our age, partly as a result of democratic sentiment, and partly because of the complexity of machine production, is in danger of carrying the doctrine of co-operativeness to lengths which will be fatal to individual excellence, not only in its more anarchic forms, but also in forms which are essential to social progress. Perhaps, therefore, even a man like Godwin may have something to teach to those who believe that social conformity is the beginning and end of virtue.

18 May 1932

Our Woman Haters

We all know the sort of woman who hates men, though as a man I rejoice that she is less common than she used to be. She proclaims her hatred on public platforms, justifies it on the highest moral ground, and considers it important that men should know of it in order that their intolerable conceit may suffer a blow – which, alas, it seldom does.

The woman-hating man is a very different type from the man-hating woman. He lacks her self-assurance, her ferocity, her lofty ethical fervour. He does not feel that he represents a cause, or, if he does, it is one that was lost before Adam and Eve left Paradise. Aware that he walks amid dreadful perils, he keeps his view to himself and shuns all contact with the alarming sex. But fate lies in waiting for him as implacably as a terrier at a rat hole: at the age of fifty or thereabouts, he falls ill and is efficiently nursed by some brawny and capable sick nurse.

When he is convalescent but still weak, she informs him that she will soon have to leave him but that she cannot imagine how he will get on without her to look after him. He cannot imagine it either; so he marries her, and she lives happily ever after.

Sometimes this type of man writes books; when he does, they are very fierce and manly. Nietzsche belonged to this category and, as everyone knows, was such a bloodthirsty author that he was accused of having caused the Great War. When he writes about 'Woman' he writes as though whole regiments of that (in his opinion) contemptible sex trembled at his slightest frown. From this every experienced woman decides that in real life he was submissive and terrified.

There is, however, another type of woman hater, rather more complex; this is the Don Juan type, who is perpetually seeking his ideal in woman, failing to find it, and abandoning the flawed idol as soon as he perceives the flaw. I confess I have little patience with this type.

Why should woman be an ideal to man any more than man to woman? Being an ideal must be dull work, involving daily hypocrisy and the constraint of unnatural behaviour. Your true Don Juan will find his faith in a lady shattered because she has a cold in her head or is not sprightly at breakfast; he never asks himself whether he is guiltless of these soul-shattering crimes.

The Don Juan type, while it believes itself very manly, is really the victim of a mother complex. Children do not know their mother, as a rule, at all completely – their mothers keep their adult concerns away from the children's notice. Children thus get a conception of a woman wholly devoted to them, having no life apart from them, destitute of that core of egoism without which life is impossible. Even those who, like Byron, have mothers who are the exact opposite of all this derive from literature and current sentiment an ideal of motherhood and unconsciously desire of a wife what they have failed to obtain from a mother.

Current sentiment in this has been at fault, though it is less so than it was formerly. The Don Juans of our days are belated specimens and cannot proclaim their woes with the self-confidence and gloating tragicality of their predecessors. Some other role is more suited to the modern age – perhaps that of psychoanalyst will be found the best.

25 May 1932

The Influence of Fathers

The influence of fathers in the present day is much less than it used to be. This is owing partly to schools and partly to the fact that men are busier than they were in former times. It has happened repeatedly in history that a man who had achieved a certain eminence in his line brought up his son to follow in his footsteps and was far surpassed by his son. Nowadays, distinguished men often have no sons, and when they have, their sons hate them, because, wherever the young men go, people say 'Oh, are you the son of the distinguished so-and-so?' with the result that personality seems lost in filial attributes. The one desire of the son, therefore, is *not* to follow in his father's footsteps but to be as different from his father as possible.

In ancient times, this sort of thing did not happen. I doubt if anyone ever said to Alexander the Great, 'Oh, are you the son of the distinguished King Philip?' Certainly if anyone ever did, Alexander must have killed him on the spot. The influence of the father in this case is psychologically interesting because emulation was combined with hatred. While Philip lived, Alexander feared that his father's victories would leave nothing for him to conquer. When Alexander was twenty, King Philip was assassinated, probably with the connivance of Alexander's mother, whom Alexander loved dearly. When he died at the age of thirty-two, he had conquered all Asia up to and including the Punjab, which left him in no doubt of having eclipsed his father's fame. Aristotle at intervals wrote him professorial letters saying 'Oh fie!' and telling him it was vulgar to take so much interest in barbarians, but Alexander only replied by sending him specimens of the flora of the Indus Valley, together with some elementary geographical information.

Many other distinguished careers have been inspired by paternal influence: Hannibal, Frederick the Great, Mozart, and John Stuart Mill may serve as examples. Love of the father is by no means necessary; what is necessary is technical instruction from an early age, direction of attention into a narrow channel, and ambition to achieve distinction which, with such an education, must be of the same kind as the father's.

The modern world scarcely affords opportunities for an education of this sort. Partly for this reason, distinguished men of the old type are growing very rare. To achieve the highest degree of distinction requires, no doubt, considerable native ability, but it requires much more than this. It requires some overmastering and rather simple passion, such as the desire to conquer the world or to avenge the wrongs of Carthage. It requires absorption from an early age in matters relevant to one kind of career. A father's influence may easily lead to these results, given the right sort of disposition in the son. In Napoleon's case, the necessary narrowness was secured by sending him to the military academy at Brienne, with the result that his whole subsequent education was concerned with war. It is not by an all-round education or by catholicity of interests that first-rate eminence is achieved: it is achieved by concentration and a certain narrowness both emotional and intellectual. In a world where all young people have the same environment, and the same standards presented for their acceptance, this does not easily happen. Diversity is necessary to distinction, and uniformity in education tends to produce mediocrity in adult life. We must therefore expect that individual eminence will be rarer in the future than it has been in the past.

1 June 1932

On Societies

One of the characteristics of the modern man, and still more of the modern woman, is the habit of belonging to organisations for all kinds of the most diverse purposes. There are societies for games and sport; I myself am vice-president of a cricket club in one place and of a football club in another, though I would die sooner than play either cricket or football.

There are societies for political purposes: those which promote Sunday games and those which combat them; those which advocate free trade and those which urge a higher tariff; those which combat war and those which promote preparedness; the anti-fascists and the British fascisti.

There are societies for social purposes that lie outside party politics, such as the preservation of footpaths or ancient monuments, the exploration of druidical remains, or the prevention of the extinction of the iguanodon.

Then there are learned societies: conchologists, egyptologists, arboreticulturists, topiarians, etc. I suppose Great Britain contains fewer societies than inhabitants, but not much fewer. I have never met an adult who did not belong to at least half a dozen.

Every meeting of every society is exactly like every meeting of every other. There is a president, a trifle richer and grander than the other members and rather less interested than the rest in the great purpose for which the society exists. There is an honorary treasurer who deprecates all expenditure and points out that all subscriptions are in arrears. There is an honorary secretary who hopes in due course to succeed the president. But none of these would suffice to keep the society alive; this is the function of the paid secretary.

I shudder to think what would become of immense numbers of intelligent and high-minded men and women who at present earn their livelihood by advocating some reform which is very unlikely to be carried, if, by some magician's stroke, all their various measures were to be achieved. The ranks of the unemployed would be swelled most dangerously. The motto of the secretary of a society should be: 'To travel hopefully is a better thing than to arrive', for arrival spells ruin. Yet the secretary must continually do his best.

I sometimes wonder whether there is a secret league or trade union of secretaries, where the secretary of the Association for Sunday Games meets the secretary of the Lord's Day Observance Guild and they decide on joint energetic campaigns of which the net result shall be zero. I wish I could think so.

But I am afraid human inertia does all that is necessary to preserve these worthy men and women from the disaster of success. The one thing they all have in common is a desire to change something, and while everybody wants *something* changed, few people want the particular change that a given society advocates. Men are marvellously impervious to propaganda.

I met once the honorary secretary of the Nut-Eaters' Brotherhood. 'Do you mean to say', she exclaimed, 'that you never heard of the paralysed consumptive in Prague who took to a diet of nuts and within a month won the heavyweight championship of Czechoslovakia?' When I protested that I had no desire to be a heavyweight champion, she deluged me with instances of men who had failed to be senior wranglers and had rashly eaten beefsteaks during their examinations. Our arboreal ancestors, it appears, lived on nuts and had amazing mathematical ability.

In spite of these arguments, I learned that only 323 persons belonged to the Brotherhood and, of these, 307 were suspected, on account of their sickly constitution, of the practice of clandestine meat-eating.

Such is our immunity to reason, acquired through long ages of natural selection.

8 June 1932

On Being Edifying[11]

We all ought, of course, to be highly virtuous, but the degree to which we ought to proclaim our own virtue depends upon our profession. A horse dealer or a bookmaker is not expected to have an air of piety, a sailor is not expected to be as nice in his diction as a family physician. The professions in which a man is allowed to behave in a natural manner are, of course, on the whole less lucrative than those in which a high standard of humbug is required. The corporation lawyer, the corrupt politician, and the popular psychiatrist are expected to utter moral sentiments with profound earnestness and great frequency, but in return for this hard work, they are allowed a suitable remuneration. There are, however, two professions in which a high standard of edification is demanded without being paid for in proportion to the moral and intellectual damage that it entails: these two are the professions of teaching and preaching. With regard to preaching, I will say nothing, since edification is of its essence, but in the teaching profession the supposed need of edification is disastrous, and we shall never get a sound population until every teacher who can be proved to have edified is dismissed on the spot.

Let us first be clear as to what edification consists of. If I say to a child: 'Do not eat deadly night shade because if you do, you will die', that is not edifying. But if I say to him: 'Do not eat too many chocolates because if you do, you will be guilty of the sin of gluttony', that is edifying. Now there was never yet a child that cared two pins whether he committed the sin of gluttony or not, though there are many who do not wish to be considered gluttons by their elders, because being disapproved of is uncomfortable. When you say to a child: 'Do not do this because it is a sin,' the meaning that you convey to the child is: 'Do not do this because if you do, I shall cause you discomfort by my disapproval and its consequences.' But this latter statement is no more edifying than the statement that the deadly nightshade will kill you. The essence of edification, in fact, is falsehood: it consists in giving a reason for something which is not the real reason.

I am not saying that all morality is humbug – far from it. For every sound piece of morality there is a sound reason which can be set forth as simply and straightforwardly as the reason for not eating deadly nightshade. But what is humbug is the notion of morality as something suspended in the air, existing for its own sake and quite independent of the consequences of our acts. Immoral acts are harmful acts, and in general there are social penalties for socially harmful acts, so that socially harmful acts are not in the interests of the individual. All this can be made plain to the young without bringing in lofty sentiments.

I am not denying that there is a morality of the heart as well as a morality of the will; there are not only good acts but good feelings. To ensure that people should have good feelings is extremely desirable, but it cannot be achieved by preaching. On the contrary, one of the effects of a belief in sin is to justify malevolence towards the sinner under the guise of a wish to bring him to repentance. When we get rid of the belief in sin, it becomes much harder to disguise our unkind feelings under a cloak of morality. The morality of the heart, as I see it, consists in the main of kindly feelings and good nature. But these cannot be produced by sermons: they are produced by good digestion, sound glands, and fortunate circumstances. 'Do your duty, however unpleasant it may be for all concerned' is edifying and appeals to your sadistic instincts. 'Eat more green vegetables, and you will hate your neighbours less' is scientific morality but is by no means edifying.

11 June 1932

On Sales Resistance

Throughout recent years, a vast amount of money and time and brains has been employed in overcoming sales resistance, i.e. in inducing unoffending persons to waste their money in purchasing objects which they had no desire to possess. It is characteristic of our age that this sort of thing is considered meritorious: lectures are given on salesmanship, and those who possess the art are highly rewarded. Yet, if a moment's consideration is given to the matter, it is clear that the activity in question is a noxious one which does more harm than good. Some hard-working professional man, for example, who has been saving up with a view to giving his family a pleasant summer holiday, is beset in a weak moment by a highly trained bandit who wants to sell him a grand piano. He points out that he has no room large enough to house it, but the bandit shows that, by knocking down a bit of wall, the tail of the piano can be made to project from the living room into the best bedroom. Paterfamilias says that he and his wife do not play the piano and his oldest daughter has only just begun to learn scales. 'The very reason why you should buy my piano' says the bandit. 'On ordinary pianos scales may be tiresome, but on mine they have all the depth of the most exquisite melody.' The harassed householder mentions that he has an engagement and cannot stay any longer. The bandit threatens to come again next day; so, in despair, the victim gives way and his children have to forgo their seaside holiday, while his wife's complaints are a sauce to every meal throughout the summer.

In return for all this misery, the salesman has a mere commission and the man whose piano is being sold obtains whatever percentage of the price represents his profit. Yet, both are thought to have deserved well of their country since their enterprise is supposed to be good for business.

All this topsy-turvydom is due to the fact that everything

ecomonic is looked upon from the standpoint of the producer rather than of the consumer. In former times, it was thought that bread is baked in order to be eaten; nowadays we think that it is eaten in order to be baked. When we spend money, we are expected to do so not with a view to our enjoyment of what we purchase but to enrich those who have manufactured it. Since the greatest of virtues is business skill and since skill is shown in making people buy what they don't want rather than what they do, the man who is most respected is the one who has caused most pain to purchasers. All this is connected with a quite elementary mistake, namely, failure to realise that what a man spends in one direction he has to save in another so that bullying is not likely to increase his total expenditure. But partly also it is connected with the notion that a man's working hours are the only important part of his life and that what he does with the rest of his time is unimportant unless it affects other men's working hours. A few clergymen, it is true, speak of the American home and the joys of family life, but that is regarded merely as *their* professional talk, against which a very considerable sales resistance has grown up. And so everything is done for the sake of something else. We make money not in order to enjoy what it provides but in order that in spending it we may enable others to make money which they will spend in enabling yet others to make money which. . . . But the end of this is bedlam.

22 June 1932

Should Children Be Happy?[12]

To make children happy is not difficult. It requires only affection, common sense, and good spirits. But I am constantly told by my friends – and not only by the highbrows among them – that those who make children happy unfit them for later life. The highbrow tells me that the world is a horrible place which can only be endured by those who have never experienced happiness and therefore do not miss it. The ordinary citizen tells me that it was not by means of happiness in his early years that he was made into the man he is. No, sir, it was by stern discipline, by the austere experience of going without, by toil and hardship and severity.

The man who says this is speaking the truth; it was no doubt by such methods that he was made into the man he is. Whether this is altogether a recommendation of the methods is, however, perhaps less certain than he thinks. Ever since the bickerings of Cain and Abel, parents have wondered what the young were coming to. Adam no doubt made a virtue of the fact that he had never killed his brother and pointed out that in his youth he was not allowed so much as one bite of an apple without getting into trouble. Such talk is mere conservatism and has too little substance to be dealt with by serious argument.

The highbrow who maintains the same position is no doubt dominated by the same motives at bottom but conceals them behind a more imposing verbal facade. He will allege that all great achievement has been the outcome of some kind of misery, and he will point out that people like the Samoans, who are said to be happy in childhood and even in adolescence, have never contributed anything to civilisation. If we were all happy, he tells us, we should rapidly sink into the condition of pigs, who, in his opinion, enjoy much more happiness than falls to the lot of intelligent people.

For my part, I cannot believe that the recipe for great achievement is as simple as all that. To make children unhappy is even easier than to make them happy, and the methods have been carried to great perfection by many generations of educational experts. If that were all, geniuses ought to be as common as blackberries. The alumni of Dotheboys Hall ought to have led the world in science and art.

In those rare cases where an unhappy person overcomes his misery sufficiently to produce great work, it is likely to be in some degree tainted by the fact that it is for him an escape from reality. Not invariably, but in a large proportion of cases, this quality of escape will cause a man's work to be lacking in robustness and sanity. Moreover, remarkable achievement is just as often harmful as beneficial. I dare say that Attila had a very unhappy childhood, though on this point history is unfortunately silent. Certainly Napoleon would have been neither so snobbish nor so bellicose if he had not in his youth suffered humiliation through poverty. If Napoleon could have been induced to be satisfied with the happiness of the pig, it would have been well for mankind. The element of cruelty in both the practice and the theory of many great men is attributable to the fact that their career, unconsciously to themselves, is their revenge upon the world for what it made them suffer in youth.

There is only one kind of unhappiness that is really fruitful, and that is the kind which springs from good things imagined but not realised. This form of unhappiness is inseparable from the creative impulse, but the creative impulse itself is only hampered and weakened by personal troubles. Such at least is my belief. The belief may perhaps be mistaken, but it cannot be proved to be so, and there is therefore no reason to curb our kindlier impulses.

June 1932

Dangers of Feminism

This article is addressed to men only – women are requested not to read it.

Have you, Sir Reader, met a really thoroughgoing feminist? In case you have not, you may do well to fortify yourself against the possibility of such an encounter in the future. The ordinary everyday feminist is content to suggest that men and women should be equals, but the thoroughgoing feminist holds that women should have the position hitherto enjoyed by men and men should have the position hitherto endured by women. Can anything so monstrous be imagined? But the justification offered is still more monstrous: it is revenge.

The first step will be the reform of language. Instead of speaking of 'man and the lower animals' we shall be taught to speak of 'woman and the lower animals'. I had occasion recently to remark on the surprising slowness of pupils in learning, and I wrote: 'The ordinary boy learns his lesson much more slowly than his teacher expects him to do.' The everyday feminist would substitute: 'The ordinary boy or girl learns his or her lesson much more slowly than his or her teacher expects him or her to do.' But the thoroughgoing feminist substitutes: 'The ordinary girl learns her lesson much more slowly than her teacher expects her to do.' In French, if you wish to speak collectively of a hundred women and one male infant, the 'they' that alludes to them is masculine, as is reasonable; but under the reformed system a collection of a hundred men and one female infant will be feminine.

From language these reformers will pass on to other measures. A man, on marrying, will lose his surname, adopting the maiden name of his wife, which will be that of their children. If, by some accident, a man inherits a fortune, he will be expected to consult female relatives or female lawyers as to its investment on the ground that men, in spite of their high moral qualities, seldom have much head for business.

I stayed once in a country house where there were three very clever young women and several young men. I overheard the former discussing the latter, and they were saying: 'Of course, they haven't much logic or power of reasoning, but they have marvellous intuition.' I doubt whether the young men would have been wholly pleased if I had reported this verdict to them; but in a thorough feminist regime they would have had to pretend that they regarded it as a compliment, for in such a regime men will have to rely for success upon their social charm, which will consist in skilfully persuading women to feel superior. The best way for a young man to get on will be to make a rich marriage, and the best way to make a rich marriage will be to ask for explanations of things so simple that even the richest women will be able to understand them. Other men, watching a young man pretending to be ingenuous, will make cynical comments about how shrewd he can be when he chooses.

It will become generally recognised that men have more interest in detail than women and higher moral standards, but that they are lacking in comprehensiveness and in the power of calm judgement. How, indeed, women will ask, could it be otherwise in view of the length of time they spend on personal adornment?

Meanwhile, fortunately, men escape these humiliations. What does it matter if women suffer them? After all, they are used to them.

6 July 1932

On Expected Emotions

If you decide to catch a certain train at a certain time on a certain day, you can do so, unless some accident intervenes. But if you decide to feel some specific emotion at some predetermined moment, you are very likely to fail. You say to yourself (we will suppose): 'At 6:23 p.m. next Saturday I will be overwhelmed by the beauty of Gray's *Elegy*.' But when the time comes you think this poem tiresome, and no exercise of willpower will make you feel otherwise.

This is an inconvenient fact which used to be ignored by all, and is still not sufficiently recognised by the old. Almost all our institutions depend, for their success, upon capacity for feeling expected emotions. We expect religious emotions in church on Sunday morning, and feel ashamed if we find ourselves looking forward to Sunday dinner. If we are old-fashioned parents, we expect our children to feel gratitude to us for their existence and to combine admiration of our wisdom with perennial amusement at our stock jokes. When they do not feel these expected emotions, we regard them as unnatural monsters. In marrying, bride and bridegroom are informed that it will henceforth be their 'duty' to love one another, although, since love is an emotion, it is not subject to the control of the will and therefore cannot come within the scope of duty. Considerate behaviour may be a duty, but love is a gift from heaven: when the gift is withdrawn, the one who has lost it is to be pitied, not blamed.

There are, it is true, some admirable men whose emotions are never unexpected. They are invariably portly, middle-aged, and dignified, respected, irreproachable, and pillars of society. I knew one highly amiable example of this type, who went to Palestine at a time when this journey was less common than it is now. Being at once prudent and economical, he arranged with his family a private telegraphic code. If he telegraphed the one word 'Bang', for example, they were to interpret it as meaning:

'Have landed at Jaffa. Am well and happy. Please send laundry.' If he telegraphed 'Pish', that was to mean: 'Your letters are neither so long nor so informative as I could wish. I desire to know whether the rhododendrons are blossoming well, and whether the weeping willow which I caused to be planted beside the lake is flourishing.' But if he telegraphed 'Grand', that was to mean: 'The flora and fauna of the Holy Land have surpassed even my expectations.' They did, and he did.

Happy man, moving in stately fashion through a well-ordered universe that never surprised him except when he expected it to do so! What peace, what calm, must have been his! But for humbler mortals these joys are impossible: they find the world unpredictable, and themselves quite unlike the flora and fauna of the Holy Land. For them, whatever assumes the permanence and predictability of emotions is liable to be a cause of unhappiness, or at least of hypocrisy. In dealing with the young, it is of great importance to remember that one must never demand an emotion. Your children, if they are fond of you, will usually show a spontaneous pleasure when you return from a journey. But it may happen that someone has just given them a dog, or that they are absorbed in a puzzle, and in that case they may be completely indifferent to your arrival. If, in these circumstances, you demand a display of emotion, you are giving a lesson in humbug. And if there is anything in which our age is better than its predecessors, it is the dislike of humbug that characterises the young.

13 July 1932

On Modern Uncertainty

There have been four sorts of ages in the world's history. There have been ages when everybody thought they knew everything, ages when nobody thought they knew anything, ages when clever people thought they knew much and stupid people thought they knew little, and ages when stupid people thought they knew much and clever people thought they knew little. The first sort of age is one of stability, the second of slow decay, the third of progress, and the fourth of disaster. All primitive ages belong to the first sort: no one has any doubt as to the tribal religion, the wisdom of ancient customs, or the magic by which good crops are to be secured; consequently everyone is happy in the absence of some tangible reason, such as starvation, for being unhappy.

The second sort of age is exemplified by the ancient world before the rise of Christianity but after decadence had begun. In the Roman Empire, tribal religions lost their exclusiveness and force: in proportion as people came to think that there might be truth in the religions of others, they also came to think that there might be falsehood in their own. Eastern necromancy was half believed, half disbelieved; the German barbarians were supposed to possess virtues that the more civilised portions of mankind had lost. Consequently everybody doubted everything, and doubt paralysed effort.

In the eighteenth and early nineteenth centuries, exactly the opposite happened. Science and scientific technique were a novelty, and gave immense self-confidence to those who understood them. Their triumphs were obvious and astonishing. Repeatedly, when the Chinese Emperor had decided to persecute the Jesuits, they would turn out to be right about the date of an expected eclipse when the imperial astronomers were wrong, and the Emperor would decide that such clever men, after all, deserved his favours. In England, those who introduced scientific methods in agriculture obtained visibly larger crops than those who adhered to old-time methods, while in manufactures steam and machinery put the conservatives to flight. There came, therefore, to be a general belief in educated intelligence. Those who did not possess it allowed themselves to be guided by those who did, and an era of rapid progress resulted.

In our age, the exact opposite is the case. Men of science like Eddington are doubtful whether science really knows anything. Economists perceive that the accepted methods of doing the world's business are making everybody poor. Statesmen cannot find any way of securing international co-operation or preventing war. Philosophers have no guidance to offer mankind. The only people left with positive opinions are those who are too stupid to know when their opinions are absurd. Consequently the world is ruled by fools, and the intelligent count for nothing in the councils of the nations.

This state of affairs, if it continues, must plunge the world more and more deeply into misfortune. The scepticism of the intelligent is the cause of their impotence, and is itself the effect of their laziness: if there is nothing worth doing, that gives an excuse for sitting still. But when disaster is impending, no excuse for sitting still can be valid. The intelligent will have to shed their scepticism, or share responsibility for the evils which all deplore. And they will have to abandon academic grumblings and peevish pedantries, for nothing that they may say will be of any use unless they learn to speak a language that the democracy can appreciate.

20 July 1932

On Imitating Heroes

A number of different sorts of motives lead people to behave otherwise than as their direct impulses would dictate. Of these, religion and morality have received the most attention, but there are others quite as powerful. There is the desire to please superiors, the desire for popularity with equals or inferiors, the desire for notoriety, and the desire to please some one special person. Of each of these many important examples could be given from history. But there is also another motive, which is common and very powerful: namely the wish to resemble some favourite character. Alexander the Great has influenced many important men. In the mind of Julius Caesar he caused despair because Alexander's conquests were completed at an age when Caesar's had scarcely begun. Julian the Apostate, when he was fighting the Persians, won a victory and had the opportunity of an advantageous peace. He refused the Persian offer because Alexander at the same stage had refused a similar offer. Alexander had gone on with the war and been victorious; Julian went on with it and was defeated. When Napoleon went to Egypt, he conceived himself as at the first stage in the conquest of the East: the lure of India drew him on, and he saw himself as Alexander's successor. After Nelson had brought his Egyptian adventure to grief, he was compelled to choose other models, such as Caesar and Charlemagne. He never ceased to dramatise himself in some historic role until in his downfall he was driven to the part of Hannibal. Plutarch's *Lives* had a profound influence upon Napoleon, as upon many previous prominent men, in providing patterns of behaviour, by following which a man could hope to achieve glory.

The imitation of a chosen hero is a powerful incentive, not only in the lives of the great but in the lives of a large proportion of ordinary men; and the imitation of a heroine plays a similar part in the lives of women. The result is often ludicrous and disastrous, especially when the model is not in real life but in romantic fiction. Heroes and heroines on the stage, and still more in the cinema, set too high a standard to the young; it is scarcely to be hoped that life will be so adventurous or so fitted with poetic justice in reality as it is in romance. When young people realise this, their imitation is apt to become confined to a world of imagination, with the result that the vivid part of their life is in daydreams, not in reality. Even disaster is better than such a divorce between emotion and action.

But not *much* better. Modern young intellectuals in England are apt to model themselves upon Mr Aldous Huxley or one of his characters, with the result that their behaviour becomes unnatural, stilted, and priggish. In a situation where some simple and straightforward action is to be expected, they suddenly remember that in some novel the hero becomes complex and philosophic at the crucial moment; this seems to them 'grand', and they force themselves to do likewise. The result is discomfort and unreality to themselves and all with whom they come in contact.

Another model, mainly though not exclusively feminine, is that of the suffering saint. Who has not known 'good' women who induced others to behave unkindly to them in order to display themselves to themselves as patient and unresisting and noble? The ministering angel is another type of 'good' woman, who, when she is imitating a model, may be very trying, always hoping for misfortunes among her friends in order that she may alleviate them with unerring skill and tact.

It seems that imitation of a hero or heroine is not a very satisfactory business. Perhaps, on the whole, it is best to put up with being the person one is.

27 July 1932

On Vicarious Asceticism

That luxury is enervating is a proposition which has been maintained by most moralists ever since the time of Diogenes. When the arguments for this point of view are advanced by a philosopher who lives in a tub, we may listen to him with respect, since obviously he himself believes them. In fact, up to a point their validity may be admitted. I have never myself tried living in a tub, which would be unpleasant except in a Mediterranean climate; but I have lived with great contentment in a labourer's cottage. The voluntary simple life, chosen in order to have leisure for interesting pursuits, has much to recommend it, and no doubt many of the rich spend more on the acquisition of material possessions than they would if they pursued happiness wisely.

But arguments against luxury have a rather different flavour when they are addressed by the rich to the poor with a view to making them contented with their lot, or even willing to accept lower wages. In the early nineteenth century, in England, all the forces of upper-class religion were devoted to persuading people that the poor could only be kept virtuous by low wages and that, since virtue is the greatest of goods, it was the duty of Christian employers to reduce wages to the utmost possible extent. The more prosperous wage earners were portrayed as monsters of wickedness because of their wealth. For example the frame-work knitters received, on the average, the princely wage of fourteen or fifteen shillings a week for working twelve or thirteen hours a day. In 1812, the Rev. J. T. Becker, who knew them well, pointed out the deplorable results:

'Abundance thus rapidly acquired by those who were ignorant of its proper application hastened the progress of luxury and licentiousness, and the lower orders were almost universally corrupted by profusion and depravity scarcely to be credited by those who are strangers to our district. Among the men the discussion of politics, the destruction of game, or the dissipation of the ale houses was substituted for the duties of their occupation during the former part of the week, and in the remaining three or four days a sufficiency was earned for defraying the current expenses.'[13]

It must not be supposed that this reverend gentleman was in any way peculiar. His point of view was that of all upper-class moralists. The only thing that produced a change was the coming of democracy: when working men acquired the vote, politicians had to speak of them with respect, and gradually this practice spread to other public utterances, though in private the rich still continued to think that the poor were corrupted by too much wealth.

There has been a similar development in regard to women. Until they had the vote, it was thought that they must enjoy, for example, abstinence from smoking. When one asks oneself what men gained by preventing women from enjoying cigarettes, one can only conclude that the power of issuing prohibitions was in itself so delightful as to cause a whole code of feminine behaviour to grow up in order that men might be able to gloat over the pleasures denied to the opposite sex.

When Gregory VII was engaged in enforcing the celibacy of the clergy, he called in the help of the laity, who, even when happily married themselves, were delighted at the opportunity of persecuting parish priests and their wives.

It is the strength of this impulse in human nature that makes democracy necessary. Democracy is desirable, not because the ordinary voter has any political wisdom, but because any section of mankind which has a monopoly of power is sure to invent theories designed to prove that the rest of mankind had better do without the good things of life. This is one of the least amiable traits of human nature, but history shows that there is no adequate protection against it except the just distribution of political power throughout all classes and both sexes.

3 August 1932

On Labelling People

While it is undoubtedly our duty to love our neighbours, it is a duty not always easily performed, and some neighbours, it must be admitted, do nothing to make it less difficult. There are many ways in which they may be irritating, but one of the worst (to my way of thinking) is that of classifying everybody with some obvious label. People who have this unfortunate habit think that they have complete knowledge of a man or woman when they have pinned on the tag that they consider appropriate. This is, I think, a predominantly feminine vice and belongs more particularly to women who entertain a great deal. The art of being a hostess must be a difficult one, seeing how many women fail at it. 'Oh Mr So-&-So,' says the hostess, 'you are *so* artistic, I am *sure* you will enjoy meeting Miss Such-&-Such, who paints such *charming* pictures.' Mr So-&-So is (we will suppose) a celebrated art critic of the most refined and exquisite taste, while Miss Such-&-Such paints simple sentimental water colours. Only the force of civilised taboos prevents their conversation from becoming a snarling expression of their mutual hatred. Another person is labelled 'musical', another 'literary', another 'fond of dogs', and so on, and each is expected to be delighted to meet anybody else with the same label.

There is, however, a fundamental opposition between the emotions of the person classified and those of the person who does the classifying. When one finds oneself summed up in an adjective, one automatically resents the idea that one's personality has so little complexity. When the gushing hostess says to me 'Oh Mr Russell, I know you are so fond of books,' I wish I could reply, with the manner of Dr Johnson, 'Madam, I never read a book when some less unprofitable manner of disposing of my time is available.' We all feel ourselves above classification. Some philosophers – Bergson, for example – have appealed to this feeling and have advanced theoretical reasons for the view that what is interesting in each of us is something that eludes verbal analysis. Philosophers who do this are very popular.

When people read the works of writers who exalt Man, they apply what is said to themselves and are accordingly pleased. If, instead, of thinking only of themselves, they were to remember that 'Man' includes Mr Brown and Mrs Jones and all the other tiresome neighbours, they would find themselves compelled either to change their view of Man, or to become more respectful in their thoughts about their acquaintances. This matter of classifying is a case in point. To suppose that a person can be adequately described by an epithet, such as 'romantic' or 'modern-minded' or 'scientific', is to suppose something disrespectful. The idea that, although oneself is full of mysterious and impenetrable depths, other people are quite easy to understand, is part of the belief in one's own superiority which most people carry about with them in spite of its statistical improbability. Like all contemptuous opinions, it makes the world seem less interesting than it really is. To understand another human being is not easy and is never achieved by those who do not know that it is difficult. But what is of most value in the study of history, in friendship, and in love is the gradual and tentative approximation to the understanding of personalities unlike one's own. This is not to be achieved by putting people in categories, nor yet by the faculty of intuition in which many people put their trust. A combination of the two is necessary but is not alone sufficient. What is most necessary of all is to avoid the cocksureness that springs from an unfounded contempt.

10 August 1932

On Smiling

All the higher animals have methods of expressing pleasure, but human beings alone express pleasure when they do not feel it. This is called politeness and is reckoned among the virtues. One of the most disconcerting things about infants is that they only smile when they are pleased. They stare at visitors with round grave eyes, and when the visitors try to amuse them, they display astonishment at the foolish antics of adults. But as soon as possible, their parents teach them to seem pleased by the company of people to whom they are utterly indifferent.

In oriental countries polite smiling has been carried to much greater lengths than among ourselves. In Japan, until 1868, a social superior had the right to kill a social inferior if he failed for an instant to keep smiling while in the great man's presence. In the family, the wife had to smile in the presence of her husband and the children in the presence of their parents. This was what made the Japanese appear to Western travellers such a cheerful people; it was a case of survival of the fittest.

But it is not always a smile that is demanded by politeness in the presence of social superiors. In Korea, for example, subjects having audience of the Emperor were expected to tremble visibly as long as his eye was upon them to show their realisation of the fact that he could put them to death if he chose. In like manner, in England a well-trained butler never smiles in the presence of his employers however ridiculous may be the things that happen to them. English politeness is not, however, in all respects similar to that of the Far East. In China, guests at a banquet used to be expected to smack their lips loudly while eating and to display, at the conclusion of the feast, the most unmistakable signs of having overeaten.

One of the most embarrassing forms of politeness in social intercourse is to be found among South American Indians. When a chief pays a visit to another chief, the remarks of the guest must be repeated exactly by the host on the ground that what the guest has said is perfect and cannot be bettered. The guest says 'I have come from the West.' The host replies 'You have come from the West.' The guest says 'I came by the river.' The host replies 'You came by the river.' After a while, the unfortunate guest cannot think of anything more to say. There is an uncomfortable silence, after which ordinary conversation becomes permissible. But the ritual must be resumed for the last half-hour before the visiting chief's departure.

White men have never had so high a conception of politeness as this, but we still consider it necessary to smile throughout a dull party so that when we get home our jaw muscles ache. Having learned to smile in order to conceal boredom, men tend to use the smile to conceal other less innocent emotions. Hamlet was impressed by his uncle's habit of smiling in order to conceal the fact that he was a murderer. I have not known many murderers, but those that I have known were somewhat addicted to smiling, so perhaps Hamlet's uncle was merely illustrating a general rule. But even if all murderers smile, it must not be inferred that all who smile are murderers. The world is gloomy enough already, and there is no need to employ bad logic to make it worse.

17 August 1932

Do Governments Desire War?

In every civilised country, all persons capable of apprehending plain facts are agreed that the next great war will, in all likelihood, bring the end of civilisation. This is in no sense a party question; it has nothing to do with economics or theology or any of the other issues that divide man. It has to do solely with the perfection of war technique, especially of the technique of attack. Aeroplanes and poison gas have made the attack much stronger than the defence and have made it easy to attack civilian populations behind the lines. If there should be a war (say) between England and France, it is to be expected that, within a few hours of its outbreak, practically all the inhabitants of London and Paris would be dead. Within a few days, all the main centres of industry would be destroyed and most of the railways would be paralysed. The population, maddened with terror, would fight with each other for stores of food, and those who were most successful would retire into lonely places, where they would shoot all who approached them. Probably within a week, the population of both countries would be halved, and the institutions which are the vehicles of their culture would be destroyed for ever.

All this is well known, and yet, incredible as it may seem, the governments show a rooted opposition to all serious attempts to prevent war. The Disarmament Conference, after long deliberation, decided merely to renew certain futile agreements which, as every one admits, will be broken on the day that war breaks out.[14] The assembled governments decided to flout the intelligence of the civilised world and to make it clear that they would do nothing whatever to make war less likely or less horrible.

Einstein, who is universally recognised as the greatest man of our age, went to Geneva during the conference to find out whether there was hope of anything being done. The conference having proved futile, Einstein and various other friends of peace, many of them eminent and highly respectable, attempted to hold a congress that should consider what intelligent people could do to save Europe from suicide. The Swiss Government refused them permission to meet in Switzerland, on the pretext that friends of peace must be Communists. The French Government proved equally unfriendly. The British Prime Minister, personally appealed to, did not even reply; apparently he is now ashamed of his honourable record in the Great War.[15]

The conclusion to be drawn from such facts is that the governments of the world, while not positively desiring war, are just as determined as they were before 1914 to obstruct every measure that is likely to prevent war. It is to be hoped that ordinary citizens will, before it is too late, acquire the common sense required to save themselves and their children from a horrible and futile death. The first step should be universal compulsory and complete disarmament, the second the creation of an international government. Armies and navies do not make for safety. The only way to be safe in the modern world is not to have the means of fighting.

Men like Einstein proclaim obvious truths about war but are not listened to. So long as Einstein is unintelligible, he is thought wise, but as soon as he says anything that people can understand, it is thought that his wisdom has departed from him. In this folly, governments take a leading part. It seems that politicians would rather lead their countries to destruction than not be in the government. A greater depth of wickedness than this it is not easy to imagine.

24 August 1932

On Corporal Punishment

The infliction of bodily injury as a punishment was formerly supported by all who theorised on the subject. In civilised communities, cutting off the ears or the tongue were not uncommon three hundred years ago. Branding was thought proper in New England, as every one knows from *The Scarlet Letter*.[16] Torture to extort confession was taken for granted. It still exists, as the Wickersham Commission discovered in investigating the 'third degree', but it is now illegal, even when practised by the agents of the law.[17] On the whole, every advance in civilisation goes with a mitigation in the severity of punishments and a diminution of physical chastisement. In spite of all the fears of the sterner moralists, gentler penal codes are usually accompanied by a lessening of crime. There is no case for corporal punishment, whether statistically or as a matter of the psychology of individual criminals.

Nevertheless, there has been, at least in England, a recrudescence of flogging as a criminal sentence. Men who, while they were schoolboys, were caned or flogged, almost invariably believe that they are the better for it. This belief itself, to my mind, is one of its bad effects. The man who, whether in adult life or in boyhood, has submitted to this sort of thing, is filled with anger, which turns him either into a furious rebel or into a man with a ferocious desire to torment other delinquents when his turn comes. The latter feeling can be justified as moral indignation, and the man who feels it never realises that it is really a desire to inflict on others what he has been made to suffer himself.

In England, certain crimes which are regarded as peculiarly odius can, when committed by men, be punished by flogging. Among such are living on the immoral earnings of women and assaults on women. The judges who order flogging display, in pronouncing sentence, an obvious pleasure, which they imagine to be virtuous but which is really a release of brutal instincts. In the London *Times* recently there was a letter from a clergyman regretting that this penalty cannot be inflicted when, in the opinion of the prison doctor, it is likely to do serious injury to health. This worthy Christian minister, after assuring the public that he is not 'bloodthirsty or particularly vindictive', argues that 'anyone who inflicts violence on other people should . . . whatever may be the state of his own health, take the full consequences.'[18] The House of Lords recently succeeded in making it possible to inflict flogging on boys for certain criminal offences; this is a natural consequence of the fact that most of their Lordships had suffered severe physical chastisement when they were at school.[19]

Indignation against crime is a natural emotion and causes men to think that severe penalties are desirable. But if the object is to prevent crime, not merely to give pleasure to those who inflict punishment, a more scientific attitude is desirable. All violence and brutality tend to provoke violence and brutality in return, not necessarily in the form of direct revenge, but rather in the form of general harshness and cruelty. A physician would not cure his patients more effectually if he were angry with them for being ill, and the criminal law is not more effective when it is inspired by anger against the criminal. The criminal presents a problem, psychological, educational, sociological and economic; this difficult problem is not best handled in a state of blind rage. All arguments for corporal punishment spring from anger, not from scientific understanding. As men become more scientific, such barbaric practices will be no longer tolerated.

7 September 1932

If Animals Could Talk

I met recently a mountain climber of considerable skill and first-rate intellect, in fact a man of international eminence in the world of learning, who somewhat surprised me by a theory to which, he said, his observations had led him. Mountains, he said, are made to be climbable: on rocks, foot-holds and hand-holds are found just at such distances as are necessary for a full-grown man. He contended that, if men were twice the size they are, existing climbs would become too easy to be interesting, but few new ones would be possible, so that mountain climbing would no longer be interesting. Apparently he believed that, in the remote geological ages when rocks were formed, they were fashioned with a view to the pleasure of those few eccentrics who like to risk their lives by walking up precipices as if they were flies. It seemed to me that the mountain goat, the ibex and the chamois might have other views on this subject. If they had a parliament, they would congratulate each other on the clumsiness of this horrid creature Man, and would render thanks that his cunning is impeded by such a clumsy body. Where they skip, he crawls; where they bound freely, he clings to a rope. Their evidence of beneficence in nature would be the opposite of the mountain climber's, and yet every bit as convincing.

There was an eighteenth-century divine who gravely maintained that rabbits have white tails for the convenience of those who wish to shoot them. What would rabbits have said to him if they could speak? Imagine the punishment that would have been inflicted on him if, in the course of some Gulliver's travels, he had come across a country where the rabbits held the government. Imagine the district attorney, a rabbit selected for his powers of eloquent invective, addressing the jury of rabbits. 'This degraded creature', he would thunder, 'who, incredible as it may appear, has been regarded with respect by his own abominable species, solemnly maintains that there is no wickedness in the wanton destruction of our noblest citizens to satisfy the gross appetites of so-called human beings. Nay, worse, he is so perverted as to suppose that our white tails, which, as every right-thinking rabbit knows, serve the purpose of aesthetic delight, were given us in order that it might be the easier to assassinate us.' I cannot doubt that the eminent divine would suffer the utmost rigour of the law.

I have often wondered what turkeys would think of Christmas if they were capable of thought. I am afraid they would hardly regard it as a season of peace and goodwill.

An eminent biologist of my acquaintance looks forward to the day when rats will hold the primacy among animals and human beings will have been deposed.

There is no impersonal reason for regarding the interests of human beings as more important than those of animals. We can destroy animals more easily than they can destroy us; that is the only solid basis of our claim to superiority. We value art and science and literature, because these are things in which we excel. But whales might value spouting, and donkeys might maintain that a good bray is more exquisite than the music of Bach. We cannot prove them wrong except by the exercise of arbitrary power. All ethical systems, in the last analysis, depend upon weapons of war.

14 September 1932

On Insularity

Men who live on islands have been much maligned by those who live on continents, and as the latter are the majority they have made their case heard more effectually than has been possible for the minority. Having just returned from an excursion to the Scillies, which are among the smallest inhabited islands in the world, I feel impelled to take up the cause of islanders in general and to argue that, whatever else they may be, they are not 'insular' in the ordinarily accepted meaning of the term.

The traditional view of the people who live on an island is that they are much less aware than other people of the existence of the rest of the world and of its manners and customs. The term grew up, I fancy, during the wars against the French Revolution and Napoleon, when Englishmen were unable to travel on the continent. Isolation due to war may produce in any country the characteristic we call 'insularity'. But in time of peace, I maintain, or even in time of war if a country has allies, islanders, especially if they live on a very small island, are less likely than other people to be what is commonly meant by 'insular'.

The men of the Scilly Isles are seafaring folk, most of whom have spent years of their lives in Asia and Africa. They can discuss intelligently the Sino-Japanese question, the Anglo-Dutch problem at the Cape, or any such matter. They are as conscious of distant times as of distant places. They know that in antiquity their islands were explored, for the sake of the tin trade, first by Phoenicians and then by Romans; that throughout the Middle Ages the islands were governed by the monks of an abbey of which ruins remain; that here the last stand against Cromwell was made after the execution of Charles I. Their territorial world is small, but the world of their thought and imagination is exceptionally large.

The man who lives in the middle of a large continent, unless he has enough money and leisure for long journeys, is brought much less in contact with alien customs and ways of living. In the great plains of Russia, a peasant hardly ever encounters anything non-Russian. Russian customs, Russian beliefs, Russian propaganda bound his horizon. It is this that makes it possible for Russia to build up a system different from that of the rest of the world.

In the centre of the American continent the same sort of thing happens. The bulk of the population feels that American ways are the only natural ways, American forms of government the natural forms of government, and American abuses only such as human nature makes inevitable. The same sort of thing would be found in the centre of China or of any large homogeneous continental area.

It would seem, therefore, that 'insularity', so far from being a characteristic of islanders, is, on the contrary, most often to be found among the inhabitants of vast inland countries. The further people live from the sea, the more 'insular' they become. Progress in civilisation has always come from seafaring nations: the Phoenicians, the Greeks, the Arabs, the Italians, the Dutch, the British, and (until the Civil War) the Americans.

Perhaps the invention of the railway, which has diminished the importance of the sea, is the ultimate cause of the decline of civilisation in recent times. If so, perhaps recovery will come through the perfecting of the aeroplane.

21 September 1932

On Astrologers

There is always something pathetic about a great and ancient tradition which has fallen on evil days. The astrologer, as one pictures him in the past, is an aged sage with a long white beard, speaking in a slow and trance-like manner, and felt by his auditors and himself to be possessed of mystical lore. In his most glorious days, he controlled the destiny of nations: among the Chaldeans, he stood to the King in the same relation as the Governor of the Bank of England now stands to the Prime Minister. In ancient Rome he was reverenced, except by a few rationalistic Emperors, who banished from the City all 'mathematicians', as they were called. The Arabs consulted them on all important occasions; the wisest men of the Renaissance believed in them, and Kepler, the great astronomer, had to become an astrologer in order to win respect and a livelihood.

Astrologers still exist; it has been my good fortune to know several. But how different they are from the magnificent beings of former times! They are, so far as I have come across them, hard-working and highly meritorious business men or women, with an aged mother or an invalid husband to support. They follow by rule of thumb the ancient formulae about the House of Life and planets in the ascendant and the rest of it, but their language is sadly modernised, and their horoscopes, instead of being inscribed cabalistically upon parchment, are neatly typed upon the best quarto typing paper. In this, they commit an error of judgement which makes it difficult to have faith in their power of deciphering the future in the stars.

Do they believe themselves in the sciences that they profess? This is a difficult question. Everything marvellous is believed by some people, and it is not improbable that professional astrologers are of this type. And even if they are aware that their own performances are largely guesswork and inferences from information obtained otherwise, they probably think that there are superior practitioners who never resort to these inferior methods. There was once a worthy man who made a vast fortune by professing to have discovered how to make gold out of sea water. He decamped to South America before it was too late and prepared to live happily ever after. Unfortunately another man professed to have made the same discovery; our friend believed in him, invested all his money in the new process, and lost every penny. This incident shows that people are often less dishonest than they might be thought to be, and probably professional astrologers are in the main honourably convinced of the truth of their doctrines.

That this should be possible is creditable to them but very discreditable to our educational system. In schools and universities information of all sorts is ladled out, but no one is taught to reason, or to consider what is evidence for what. To any person with even the vaguest idea of the nature of scientific evidence, such beliefs as those of astrologers are of course impossible. But so are most of the beliefs upon which governments are based, such as the peculiar merit of persons living in a certain area, or of persons whose income exceeds a certain sum. It would not do to teach people to reason correctly, since the result would be to undermine these beliefs. If these beliefs were to fade, mankind might escape disaster, but politicians could not. At all costs, therefore, we must be kept stupid.

28 September 1932

On Protecting Children from Reality

One of the firmest beliefs of parents, law-givers, and teachers in many nursery schools is that children should be preserved from all contact with crude fact and should have everything presented to them in a pretty-pretty, fanciful form. I know women who teach music to young children and instead of giving the notes their proper names, they call a crotchet 'ta', a quaver 'teh', and a semi-quaver 'ta-teh'. They have a notion that these names are more attractive to the young, though, so far as I have observed, this belief is wholly unfounded. Modern children's stories suffer from an analogous defect: they do not present a realm of fancy as such but give an air of silliness to what they pretend is real. In graver matters, there is the same error: historical characters are portrayed as wholly virtuous unless they are recognised villains. It is not thought good for the young to know that great men have their weaknesses or that great causes have always had their bad sides. Sex instruction for the young is frequently advocated, but hardly any one advocates straightforward truthfulness about the emotional and social aspects of sex. Children are taught what the flowers do and what the bees do and what men and women (according to the conventional code) ought to do. They are given no hint that, while the flowers and bees really do what they are supposed to do, men and women as a rule do not. In spite of the reaction against Victorian prudery, hardly any one sees any harm in this form of lying.

My own experience of children has led me to a quite different view. Children enjoy fancy when it is pure, that is to say, when it makes no pretence to be reality, but they distinguish sharply between fancy and fact. The person who offers them pretty fairy tales as if they were fact rouses their indignation as soon as they find out the trick that has been played on them. So long as their personal circumstances are happy, they are not readily upset by disagreeable truths concerning the world in general. They have a dislike of humbug, which usually disappears in later life. The habit of screening them from the knowledge of disagreeable truths is not adopted for their sakes although adults may think it is; it is adopted because adults themselves find candour painful.

One of the worst defects of modern education is its indifference to reality. I do not mean by 'reality' anything profound or metaphysical; I mean merely plain matters of fact. The habit of shying away in terror from every unpleasant feature of the world is a dangerous one and is the mark of a certain frivolous weakness. We are apt to imagine that, in this respect, we are better than our grandparents, but in this, I think, we flatter ourselves. We are slightly less reticent in sexual matters but far more reticent in politics. The statesmen of fifty or sixty years ago were in many ways abominable, but they were not quite such humbugs as are a large proportion of their modern successors. Perhaps those educators who take such pains to prevent children from hearing the truth about anything are hoping that they will adopt politics as a career and are trying to teach them how not to know what is inconvenient. If so, they may be justified from the standpoint of the personal success of their pupils. But the politician who shuns reality is produced by a democracy which has the same characteristic, and the community as a whole risks disaster when it refuses to know unpleasant facts.

5 October 1932

The Decay of Intellectual Standards

Modern life is adapted to labour-saving devices. We move by mechanical traction instead of by the muscles of horses; we use elevators and escalators in place of our own legs; the cook uses powders out of a tin and gives notice if asked to make soup in the old way. In former times the labour of ploughing and reaping was very severe and was celebrated in verse by poets who were exempt from honest toil; nowadays, the ploughman sits at his ease on a machine. All that part of human labour which consists in altering the position of matter in space has become immeasurably less irksome than it used to be. In comparison with the past, modern life, from a muscular point of view, is one long holiday.

There is a tendency to expect the same diminution of effort in intellectual matters. The hard work of school was formerly taken for granted since it was assumed that all work must be hard. Nowadays, there is the opposite feeling, that all work ought to be easy. A great deal of school work, it is true, used to be made unnecessarily difficult by bad methods of teaching. But however excellent the methods of teaching may be, there is much that cannot be learned without severe effort on the part of the pupil. Many modern educators resent this fact and tend to undervalue those parts of scholastic training that cannot be made easy. I do not know how it may be in America, but in England school inspectors report that arithmetical work, for example, is less accurate than it was thirty years ago. This particular change is not to be regretted since elementary schools in England have always been inclined to lay too much stress on arithmetic. But in other directions the decay of accuracy is more serious.

A simple experiment will enable the reader to judge the accuracy of his friends. Ask them the titles of the books they have read during the last few months, and you will find, almost invariably, that they make mistakes. They will make mistakes about the names and addresses of their acquaintances, except those they know very well. Whenever a fact is just so and is not a matter of sentiment or opinion, you will find that it is not accurately remembered. This is connected with the 'soft' character of modern education. Most of what was formerly taught was useless in itself but had the merit of teaching accuracy. What is taught in up-to-date schools is often worth knowing on its own account but is usually taught in such a way that the pupils do not know it at the end. The consequence is that adults have slipshod habits of mind and cease to notice distortions of fact which have a sinister motive.

The modern youth who intends to adopt a profession tends to be idle at school and only to begin hard work when he embarks upon technical training. In law school or medical school he exerts himself to acquire knowledge because it has for him an obvious economic utility. But in the earlier years of his so-called education he has managed to remain ignorant. A few boys and girls like the acquisition of knowledge, but they are exceptional.

I think educational reformers have perhaps, in a reaction against the foolish severity of the past, overlooked the fact that it is every man's duty to work and that youth cannot be regarded solely as a time for play but must also have its serious side as preparation for adult work. If youth is all play, work will afterwards be resented. And, in particular, the modern world, being more complex than the world of former times, demands more intellectual training of the citizen. The decay of intellectual standards is therefore doubly unfortunate and is certainly one of the causes of the bad state of the world.

19 October 1932

Pride in Illness

Human nature has many curious traits, but one of the most curious is pride in illness. No one thinks it a fine thing to have a motor car that is perpetually going out of order: people do not boast that after a long run their car is completely useless for several weeks, or that it is perpetually developing strange troubles which even the most skilful mechanics cannot put right. Yet that is just how people feel about their own bodies. To have a body that does its work satisfactorily is felt to be uninteresting and rather plebeian. A delicate digestion is almost indispensable in the equipment of a fine lady; in all ranks of life, it is thought a source of pride to have suffered grave danger to life in maternity. I am aware in myself of the impulse to boast of illness: I have only been ill once, but I like people to know how *very* ill I was that once, and I feel vexed when I come across other people who have been more nearly dead without dying.

This pride in illness is one of the causes of imaginary ailment. Some people, despairing of rendering themselves interesting by their conversation or their achievements, develop mysterious troubles as to which they consult large numbers of specialists, who, if they have tact without honesty, flatter the patient by saying that diagnosis surpasses their competence. These people are extreme cases, but in a lesser degree the same sort of thing is common.

It is interesting to observe the attitude which people who are proud of their physical defects take up towards their children. Some regard their children as competitors for the glory of invalidism; these people are furious when their children profess to be ill, and treat them with the harshness with which they themselves ought to be treated. It is a painful spectacle to see a healthy mother who believes herself to be on the point of death torturing an unhealthy child whom she persists in regarding as perfectly well.

The child, let us say, has rheumatism, but the mother is indignant when this is suggested. 'Rheumatism! Nonsense. Children don't have rheumatism. Growing pains, that's what it is.' No amount of medical information to the contrary will shake this type of mother; it is utterly useless to tell her that 'growing pains' is nothing but a phrase invented by selfish parents to save themselves the bother of noticing when their children are ill. The same sort of thing may happen with heart trouble, which the same type of parent will probably regard as indigestion brought on by eating too many good things.

There is, however, another type of parent, perhaps commoner nowadays, whose pride in illness includes her children's illnesses. This type of parent is endlessly fussy about the children, informing everyone who will listen that they are nervously high-strung, liable to have every cold turn into pneumonia, and only preserved from agonies of indigestion by an extraordinarily careful and scientific diet. The ordinary games and pleasures of children terrify this type of parent. The children, if they are healthy in mind and body, react by secret rebellion and probably do things far worse for their health than they would if they were sensibly treated. It is lucky if they do not let themselves down by a rope from their bedroom window on frosty nights and run about out of doors in pyjamas. But if the children have any tendency to softness, they will become mollycoddles and ultimately hypochondriacs.

Both these opposite mistakes come of regarding illness as a fine thing. Both would be avoided if people would regard human bodies as they regard motor cars, scientifically but without excessive emotion.

26 October 1932

On Charity

There are few ways in which the moral sentiments of intelligent people have changed more than as regards what is called 'charity'. It is difficult to refuse money to a beggar if his need seems genuine, but the act of giving is uncomfortable and inclined to cause a blush: there is inevitably the reflection that society ought to be so organised as to make it unnecessary for anyone to beg. So far from feeling self-satisfied because of giving, we feel our social conscience pricked because we profit by a system which reduces others to such want and humiliation.

This feeling is entirely modern. Throughout the Middle Ages, alms-giving was inculcated as a duty, with the result that numbers of sturdy beggars lived in idleness. The mendicant friars, at first, owed to the same cause the possibility of subsisting in spite of their vow of poverty. In India, down to the present day, many holy men live on the alms of the faithful, because anything so mundane as earning one's living is incompatible with the life of saintly contemplation.

In England, feudalism in decay developed a less simple form of charity as a salve to its conscience. The aristocracy, which held all political power from 1688 to 1832, spent the last half of that period in making laws which reduced wage earners to the most abject poverty, so that the condition of the people, from having been comfortable, became one of appalling wretchedness. And yet, throughout this time, the great families imagined themselves to be actuated by the most genuine benevolence towards their dependents. Greville, who lived on intimate terms with all the magnates of his day, reflects in his journal the moral outlook of his friends. 'Lady Cowper and her daughters', he says in 1832, 'inspect personally the cottages and condition of the poor. They visit, enquire, and give; they distribute flannel, medicines, money, and they talk to and are kind to them, so that the result is a perpetual stream flowing from a real fountain of benevolence, which waters all the country round and gladdens the hearts of the peasantry, and attaches them to those from whom it emanates.'[20] He conveniently forgets that, only eighteen months before, the hearts of the peasantry had been 'gladdened' to the point at which they took to rioting and rick-burning, for which some were hanged and many sentenced to transportation for life.

A few years later, after describing a banquet given by the Duke of Rutland to his 'retainers', he says:

'I should like to bring the surly Radical here who scowls and snarls at "the selfish aristocracy who have no sympathy with the people", and when he has seen these hundreds feasting in the Castle, and heard their loud shouts of joy and congratulation, and then visited the villages around, and listened to the bells chiming all about the vale, say whether "the greatest happiness of the greatest number" would be promoted by the destruction of all the feudality which belongs inseparably to this scene, and by the substitution of some abstract political rights for all the beef and ale and music and dancing with which they are made merry and glad even for so brief a space.'[21]

The money spent by the Duke in this merry-making was obtained by taxing grain so heavily that bread was at famine prices, and vast numbers of the poor died of hunger.

A hundred years ago, in a society now extinct, the point of view which puts charity above independence now seems to us grotesque. But in newer forms it still survives and is still politically powerful. It is this very same outlook which makes large numbers of people think it better that the unemployed should be kept alive by private benevolence than that they should have the legal right to support by the public authorities. In a just world, there would be no possibility of 'charity'.

2 November 1932

On Reverence

Admiration of great men, both of our own time and of the past, is a valuable emotion and a stimulus to useful activity. To young men of vigour and enterprise, the achievements of predecessors are an encouragement and a proof of what is possible to achieve.

But if this good effect is to result from admiration, it is necessary that the men who are admired should be regarded as something that it is possible to equal by means of sufficient exertion, not as something outside our capacity. It is possible to use the great men of the past as an excuse for laziness, by assuming that what they thought was perfect for all time and need never be re-examined.

This attitude is defended by those who adopt it, who call it 'reverence' and condemn all modern initiative as disrespectful. 'Reverence' in this sense has been a misfortune to the human race.

One of the most outstanding examples of the harm done by excessive reverence is the influence of Aristotle. For a brief period, in the eleventh and twelfth centuries, when the West rediscovered him through contact with the Arabs, his writings acted as an intellectual stimulus. But very soon he became the canon of orthodoxy, and no advance could be made except by showing the falsehood of what he had said.

Galileo could not induce professors of astronomy to look through his telescope at Jupiter's moons, because they knew from Aristotle that Jupiter has no moons. Throughout Galileo's life he was as much criticised for disagreeing with Aristotle as for his supposed conflict with the Scriptures.

Two centuries later, when Darwin published *Origin of Species*, he was met by dogmatic assertion of Aristotle's doctrine that each species was separately created. In logic and aesthetics his influence has been, and still is, exceedingly pernicious.

In the main, however, Aristotle's influence belongs to the past.

But the attitude of appealing to the authority of great men as unquestionable has by no means disappeared. Every young man or young woman whose opinions are not on all points those of the older generation is met with arguments inspired by this point of view. 'Do you think you are wiser than so-and-so?' says the indignant parent or teacher. 'So-and-so' is almost always a man who himself disagreed with his parents and teachers, but this fact is ignored. 'So-and-so' lived in other circumstances and necessarily did not know all sorts of things that are known nowadays. Even if 'So-and-so' was just as wise as conservatives suppose, that is no reason for supposing that his opinions are to be accepted as a guide in the circumstances of the present day.

There is no subject upon which the opinions of a man who lived long ago can be accepted as dogmas absolving us from the necessity of fresh consideration in the light of our modern environment. Not infrequently, however, men who have acquired great authority never were very wise, even in their own day. One way of being thought wise is to defend current prejudices in glowing and eloquent language so that rhetoric conceals the lack of reasoning power and the failure of sympathetic understanding.

Great writers and great orators have done incalculable harm in this way. If eloquence could be made illegal, the dangers of popular government would be much less than they are. As, however, this solution is impossible, the only way out lies in an educational system which cultivates an inquiring and scientific outlook. Perhaps, after another two or three centuries, this way out may be tried.

9 November 1932

On Proverbs

I have often wondered who invented the proverbs that everyone knows, and whether they sprang ready made from the brain of one individual or were the product of a long evolution.

As we know them, they are remarkable for their terseness. 'More haste, less speed', for example, could not possibly be said in fewer words. If a modern man of science wished to express this idea he would say (at least if he were a behaviourist): 'In locomotion the rate of diminution of the distance from a given point is inversely proportional to the average velocity,' which is cumbrous, unintelligible and untrue. If an eighteenth-century literary man (say, Dr Johnson) had wished to express what the proverb conveys in four monosyllables he would have said something like this: 'Cogitative endeavours to promote celerity of ambulation not infrequently produce retardation of the desired propinquity to the goal.'

I think we must admit that, as against science and literature, the proverb holds its own.

Nevertheless, the proverb is dying out. It belongs essentially to a stable agricultural community. Sancho Panza produced more proverbs than any other character in fiction; next to him Sir Walter Scott's Lowlanders. No one invents new proverbs, and there are no proverbs applying to modern inventions. People say, 'Take care of the pence and the pounds will take care of themselves,' but they don't say, 'Take care of the radio and the gramophone will take care of itself,' which would not be any more foolish.

The supposed wisdom of proverbs is mainly imaginary. As a rule, proverbs go in pairs which say opposite things. The opposite of 'More haste, less speed' is 'A stitch in time saves nine.' The opposite of 'Take care of the pence and the pounds will take care of themselves,' is 'Penny wise, pound foolish.' The opposite of 'Two heads are better than one,' is 'Too many cooks spoil the broth.' And so on.

The great advantage of a proverb in argument is that it is supposed to be incontrovertible, as embodying the quintessential sagacity of our ancestors. But when once you have realised that proverbs go in pairs which say opposite things you can never again be downed by a proverb; you merely quote the opposite.

Proverbs are an example of the tyranny of literary form. Two hundred years ago it was thought that whatever could be said in Latin must be true. Quotations from Shakespeare have something of the same polemic force. But proverbs are the supreme case of this sort of thing. Considered as guides to conduct, they are worthless, but from a stylistic point of view there is much to be said for them, and without this literary merit they would not be felt to have so much argumentative force.

The modern analogue of the proverb usually takes the form of slang. Slang also is anonymous in origin and is diffused orally because it satisfies a need. As it does not have to support the weight of literary tradition, it is able to speak of modern things and to draw its metaphors from the most recent inventions. Much of it, fortunately, climbs up gradually into received usage. If this were not the case the literary language would become dead, and it would soon be impossible to speak of the modern world in terms that stylists would permit.

Language, like every other social institution, requires a conflict between the conservative and the revolutionary, and the revolutionary in language is the inventor of slang.

16 November 1932

On Clothes

One of the most curious changes in manners during the last two hundred years is the decay of splendour in men's attire. From the beginning of civilisation until toward the end of the eighteenth century rich men displayed their wealth in rich garments, as their wives still do. Pepys, in the time of Charles II, spent far more on his own clothes than on those of his wife. It is an entirely modern custom that only women should dress expensively.

Nowadays men's suits, especially in the evening, are so rigidly controlled by convention as to be practically a uniform, and the slightest departure in the direction of the ornate is frowned upon. In former days, men behaved as most women still do; they spent as much on their clothes as they could afford, and they were able to display individual taste in the choice of picturesque magnificence.

To say what brought about the change is not easy. In England Puritanism had a good deal to do with it, especially as reinforced by Wesley. On the Continent the French Revolution made fine clothes dangerous: men who wore knee-breeches were liable to have their heads cut off. I suppose that those who first adopted trousers in order to save their lives during the Reign of Terror stuck to them afterward because they were comfortable.

In the nineteenth century the substitution of plutocracy for aristocracy made the change permanent; fine clothes are difficult to combine with work, and plutocrats, unlike aristocrats, usually spend part of their day in offices.

One result, which is perhaps temporary, has been a greater difference between men and women than existed in former days. The way for a man to secure the admiration of women is to distinguish himself in athletics or by a forceful personality or by an unusually successful career. Formerly a man could, as a woman still can, secure the favourable attention of the opposite sex by beautiful clothes enhancing natural good looks. It is true that feats of arms were always useful in this respect, but Shakespeare's Hotspur could complain that they were not as useful as a good perfume. The fact is that the admired aristocrats of former times were far less 'manly' than (say) a successful airman of the present day.

The decay of clothes as a source of social prestige has had the effects of making men more energetic and more enterprising than the rich men of more splendid epochs. The early feminists were right in thinking that, if women were to compete with men in men's pursuits, they would be wise to eschew fine attire. If all women wore a drab and serviceable uniform it may be assumed that the qualities for which men admire women would be more similar than they are to the qualities for which, at present, women admire men.

It must be confessed that men's standard in women is more frivolous than women's standard in men. This is regrettable but not easily to be prevented. I suppose the method of the French Revolution could be applied. If all well-dressed women had their heads cut off the survivors might set a new fashion of dowdiness. But I do not see men readily taking the lead in such a revolution, nor can I wish that they should, though something of the sort, one gathers, has happened in Russia.

This is one of the many respects in which love of beauty conflicts with social conscience. The conflict is an awkward one, and I, for one, do not know how it should be resolved.

23 November 1932

Should Socialists Smoke Good Cigars?

The man whose opinions are in any way unusual is frequently confronted by moral problems which do not trouble other people. If he were left to the dictates of his own conscience he might find summary ways of dealing with such questions, but he is constantly launched upon arguments with kind friends who say, 'Oh, I should have thought *you* ought not to do that.'

There is a great deal of confusion of thought in the average man's view as to what ought to be done by people whose opinions differ from his own. The question that I have put at the head of this article may serve as an example. My own practice in this matter, I may as well confess, is not guided by any lofty ethical principle. I seldom smoke good cigars, but that is because I cannot afford them; I never refuse one that is offered to me.

Many people would find this procedure too simple and natural for an advocate of social justice. They will say to me: 'If you believe that the world's goods ought to be divided equally among the world's inhabitants, what justification can you have for taking more than your share?'

If I took this argument seriously, I should have to estimate the total income of the world and divide it by the total number of inhabitants, and whatever might be the answer to this sum I should have to say, 'This is going to content me; anything above this I will give away.'

There are, however, several points to be considered before adopting this somewhat drastic resolution. The peasants of India and China form about half the population of the world and have an income of about £1 a year; many of the natives of Africa have even less. I doubt, therefore, whether the present average income per head throughout the world is more than about £5 a year. I rather doubt whether the attempt to live upon this sum would increase my efficiency as a propagandist; for even if by the practice of Yoga I learned to live without food, I should still not be able to pay for the paper, ink, and pen required in producing books.

Perhaps I am mistaken in this; it may be that there is room for a modern Diogenes. Perhaps if I lived in a tub, the stunt would cause me to be interviewed by all persons passing by, and it may be that in the end I should convert all with whom I spoke, though I rather doubt it. Even so, my success as a modern Diogenes would depend on my not having imitators. If socialists took to living in the deserts like early Christian hermits, they would cease to be interesting and would lose all influence upon the course of events.

The man who desires to convert others to his opinions has two courses open to him. He may make spectacular appeals to the emotions by announcing the intention of starving himself to death or, as one of the suffragettes did, by perishing beneath the hoofs of the horses at the Derby. This method can be used for the advocacy of any opinion, no matter what. But if an opinion has solid intellectual reasons in its favour, it is possible to adopt an intellectual method of propaganda.

Galileo persuaded mankind that the earth goes round the sun just as effectually as he would have done if he had made himself a martyr to the Inquisition. On the whole, the man who has an intellectually good case is well advised to make an intellectual appeal since the outcome is a more stable belief than any to be obtained by mere emotionalism.

To take a quite different point, the socialist should not appear to advocate a world in which the *present* wealth is evenly divided. It is an essential part of his case that by a more sensible organisation, the wealth of the world could be enormously increased. In the socialist millennium we shall all be able to enjoy a good cigar now and then.

30 November 1932

A Sense of Humour

'Whatever may be said against me, no one can say that I haven't got a sense of humour.' This is a speech which one hears over and over again; indeed it might be made by almost any English-speaking person. You may question all sorts of things about a man without making him really angry. You may say that he is stupid, that he is ruthless, that he is not honest about money, that he allowed his aged mother to starve in a garret, and he will argue with you calmly and reasonably to prove that he is innocent of these various crimes. But if you say that he has no sense of humour you will invariably produce an explosion of fury. This is a peculiarity of our age. In the seventeenth century, men burned each other at the stake for minute points of theology and killed each other with rapiers to prove that they were men of honour. They prided themselves, not on humour but on common sense. Descartes, who lived in that age, remarks that no quality is so well distributed as common sense, for no man has so little but that he thinks he has enough. In our time one might say the same of the sense of humour.

In the early days of the nineteenth century, when railways were being substituted for stage coaches and factory chimneys for water mills, when the beauty of the countryside was being defaced and utilitarianism ruled the world, men prided themselves upon their exquisite sensibility. In those days the necessary equipment of a gentleman was Byronic despair, a tortured heart, a love of rocky solitudes and ruined temples. He was not expected to laugh, unless it were a hollow laugh wrung from the anguish of despair. Gradually, however, these heights of sentiment were found fatiguing, and in their place came the modern cult of humour. I am not sure that the change has made the world more amusing. Where formerly ladies learnt to play the harp, they now learn to say everything with a sprightly air, and an appearance of wit. When people say to me: 'I always think the autumn is so much cooler than the summer. Ho! Ho! Ho!' and expect me to behave as though I had heard an epigram worthy of Talleyrand, I find the appropriate behaviour somewhat difficult. Even at a slightly higher level, too much humour may become very tiresome. I was once in the company of a number of professors who were talking university politics and describing various people as respectively liberals and conservatives in economic matters. I inquired, with a real desire for knowledge, what were the differences between the two university parties. The professors, each in turn, fired off a witty remark, but from none of them could I obtain any information. If I had been adequately endowed with a sense of humour, I should not have minded this, but, alas, I am that extremely rare being, a man without a sense of humour. I had not suspected this painful fact until the middle of the War, when the British War Office sent for me and officially informed me of it. I gathered that if I had had my proper share of a sense of the ludicrous, I should have been highly diverted at the thought of several thousand men a day being blown to bits, which, I confess to my shame, never caused me even to smile.

There was once a Chinese emperor who constructed a lake full of wine and drove peasants into it to amuse his wife with the struggles of their drunken drownings. He had a sense of humour.

7 December 1932

Love and Money

When the Romantic Movement was still in its first fervour, it was a common matter of debate whether people should marry for love or for money. The young people concerned usually favoured love, and their parents usually favoured money. In the novels of the period the dilemma was felicitously solved by the discovery, on the last page, that the apparently penniless heroine was really a great heiress. But in real life young men who hoped for this denouement were apt to be disappointed. Prudent parents, while admitting that their daughters should marry for love, took care that all the young men they met should be rich. This method was sometimes very successful; it was adopted, for example, by my maternal grandfather, who had a large number of romantic daughters, none of whom married badly.

In these days of psychology the matter no longer looks so simple as it did eighty years ago. We realise now that money may be the cause, or part of the cause, of quite genuine love; of this there are notable examples in history. Benjamin Disraeli, who became Lord Beaconsfield, was, in his youth, poor and struggling and passionately ambitious. He married a rich widow, much older than himself, and considered by the world to be rather silly. Owing to her, he was able to make his career a success. A cynical world naturally assumed that he loved her money better than he loved her, but in this the world was mistaken; throughout the whole of their married life, he was deeply and genuinely devoted to her. I do not suppose he would have loved her if she had been poor when he first knew her, but the gratitude which he felt for the help which he owed to her kindly interest in him easily developed into a sincere affection. A great deal of affection is based upon the fact that its object is a help in realising the purposes of the person who feels it. Men in whom ambition is the leading passion are likely to love women who assist them in their career, and it would be very shallow psychology to suppose that the love is not real because it has its instinctive root in self-interest.

An even more notable instance than Disraeli is Mohammed. As everyone knows, he was camel-driver to a rich widow whom he loved and ultimately married. It was her capital which supported him throughout the early unremunerative years of the prophet business. Mohammed was not the man to give an exclusive devotion to any one woman, but there is no doubt that, within the limit set by polygamy, he was genuinely fond of his wife and benefactress.

I have taken examples where the man was poor and the woman rich, but in a world dominated by men the opposite is the commoner case. The psychology, however, is much the same. If a very rich man asks a very poor girl to marry him, she is likely, especially if she has social ambitions, to feel a kind of gratitude which will lead her to fall in love with him, provided he is not too repulsive; at any rate, he will need a smaller degree of personal attractiveness than a poor man would need.

To him that hath shall be given; wealth can often purchase not only the semblance of love but its reality. This is unjust and undesirable but nonetheless a fact.

14 December 1932

Interest in Crime

There are some who think that a virtuous man is one who causes more happiness than misery to the world by his conduct. This view, however, will not bear a moment's examination. Of the many weighty and abstract arguments against it which have been adduced by metaphysicians, I will say nothing. It is a more homely consideration that has led me to adopt the opposite view. Consider a sensational murderer, a man, let us say, who murders a solitary and elderly miser, buries him in his garden, and is ultimately convicted by means of small particles of clay adhering to the soles of his boots. Such a man does more to further human happiness than falls to the lot of most philanthropists. I am thinking not only of the miser's heirs, or of the detectives who win promotion by bringing the crime home to its perpetrator; I am thinking of all the millions of family circles throughout the civilised world who for a moment forget their bickerings and boredoms in the excitement of a sensational case. Few things stir the heart of the public so much. Meanwhile the poor murderer, who has provided all this innocent happiness, wins none of the gratitude which should seem to be his due. Perhaps there might be some difficulty in rewarding him since this might make murders so common as to be uninteresting, but I think at least a statue might be put up to him after his execution to commemorate his disinterested public service. (I do not suggest that this should be done in Chicago, as the open spaces in that city are insufficient.)

The reason for the universal interest in sensational crime is a little obscure. I think it is made up of two parts: one is the pleasure of the hunt, and the other the imaginative release in the minds of those who would like to commit murders but dare not. I am afraid the pleasure of the hunt is a stronger element in human nature than most people are willing to recognise: it plays its part in all popular outbursts of moral indignation. Among the head-hunters of Borneo it is indulged without the need of any moral claptrap, but civilised people cannot adequately enjoy the indulgence of their baser passions until they have cloaked them in a garment of lofty ethical sentiments. When people let loose upon a murderer the savage impulses of the head-hunter, they feel neither savage nor wicked but believe themselves to be upholders of virtue and good citizenship.

The other motive for interest in crime, namely that of sympathy for the criminal, has to remain more secret and unconscious, but I think it nevertheless plays its part. But for the pressure of the law, the impulse to murder would, I think, be commoner than most people realise. In rough frontier communities, where homicide is apt to go unpunished, it becomes surprisingly common. Our great grandfathers fought duels, and it is not to be supposed that human nature has changed in any fundamental way since their time. The civilised man's behaviour is milder than his impulses so that uncivilised behaviour on the part of others gives him a vicarious satisfaction.

From this point of view detective stories fulfil a useful function. For the imaginative satisfaction of the ordinary law-abiding citizen, a murder in a book will do almost as well as a real murder. My intellectual friends, most of whom are passionate readers of detective stories, assure me that what they like is the ingenuity of the plot and the detection. But I think they are mistaken in this. We do not thoroughly enjoy the artistic execution of a performance if we have no instinctive interest in its fundamental purpose. Either the murderer or the detective must make some appeal to our emotions if we are to enjoy to the full even the most ingenious story of crime. When we all become as virtuous in our unconscious as we are in our outward behaviour, I think the interest in detective stories will cease. Meanwhile those who make a living by writing them need not feel any undue alarm, as the change is not likely to be brought about in our lifetime.

21 December 1932

How to Become a Man of Genius

If there are among my readers any young men or women who aspire to become leaders of thought in their generation, I hope they will avoid certain errors into which I fell in youth for want of good advice. When I wished to form an opinion upon a subject, I used to study it, weigh the arguments on different sides, and attempt to reach a balanced conclusion. I have since discovered that this is not the way to do things. A man of genius knows it all without the need of study; his opinions are pontifical and depend for their persuasiveness upon literary style rather than argument. It is necessary to be one-sided, since this facilitates the vehemence that is considered a proof of strength. It is essential to appeal to prejudices and passions of which men have begun to feel ashamed and to do this in the name of some new ineffable ethic. It is well to decry the slow and pettifogging minds which require evidence in order to reach conclusions. Above all, whatever is most ancient should be dished up as the very latest thing.

There is no novelty in this recipe for genius; it was practised by Carlyle in the time of our grandfathers, and by Nietzsche in the time of our fathers, and it has been practised in our own time by D. H. Lawrence. Lawrence is considered by his disciples to have enunciated all sorts of new wisdom about the relations of men and women; in actual fact he has gone back to advocating the domination of the male which one associates with the cave dwellers. Woman exists, in his philosophy, only as something soft and fat to rest the hero when he returns from his labours. Civilised societies have been learning to see something more than this in women; Lawrence will have nothing of civilisation. He scours the world for what is ancient and dark and loves the traces of Aztec cruelty in Mexico. Young men, who had been learning to behave, naturally read him with delight and go round practising cave-man stuff so far as the usages of polite society will permit.

One of the most important elements of success in becoming a man of genius is to learn the art of denunciation. You must always denounce in such a way that your reader thinks that it is the other fellow who is being denounced and not himself; in that case he will be impressed by your noble scorn, whereas if he thinks that it is himself that you are denouncing, he will consider that you are guilty of ill-bred peevishness. Carlyle remarked: 'The population of England is twenty millions, mostly fools.' Everybody who read this considered himself one of the exceptions, and therefore enjoyed the remark. You must not denounce well-defined classes, such as persons with more than a certain income, inhabitants of a certain area, or believers in some definite creed; for if you do this, some readers will know that your invective is directed against them. You must denounce persons whose emotions are atrophied, persons whose perceptions are limited, persons to whom only plodding study can reveal the truth, for we all know that these are other people, and we shall therefore view with sympathy your powerful diagnosis of the evils of the age.

Ignore fact and reason, live entirely in the world of your own fantastic and myth-producing passions; do this whole-heartedly and with conviction, and you will become one of the prophets of your age.

28 December 1932

On Old Friends

When one is no longer young there is a quite special pleasure in meeting people with whom one was friends long ago and in recalling the doughty deeds of those ancient times. Once in the course of my travels over the Western Hemisphere, I met unexpectedly, as I stepped out of the train, a man whom I had not seen for forty years, with whom I had passed a great part of my boyhood. We plunged instantly into reminiscences of people and events which I had not thought of for a generation, and I observed that we both derived special gratification from incidents showing what naughty boys we had been. He remembered more of our misdemeanours than I did, and I was much relieved to find that I had not been a goody-goody, Sunday-school pet.

Nothing is more boring to the onlooker than common reminiscences of old fogies. There is a curious pride in the most commonplace incidents of their long-ago youth, which is merely ridiculous and annoying to those whose youth is less distant. Why there should be this pride it is a little hard to say, but I think it comes of the universal desire to be many-sided. When a man has been for many years accustomed to taking the chair on public occasions, being pompous and grave and weighty, and uttering well-considered words on matters of national importance, he finds it a relief to remember that there was a time when he was different, when he could be gay and irresponsible and full of pranks. 'You see,' he says to himself, as these reminiscences pour into his mind, 'you are not at heart a tedious old bigwig; at heart you are still a boy, and if your public position permitted it, you could still engage in harum-scarum escapades.' As these thoughts pass through his mind, he begins to think himself more lovable than he seemed, and he reflects what a nicer person he is than anyone could know who only sees him performing his duties to the community.

But this is only a part, and not perhaps the most important part, of the pleasure derived from reminiscing with old friends. Another element of this pleasure is that it diminishes loneliness. As we get older the portions of our life that do not enter into our ordinary relations become greater and greater. Most of our friends know nothing of large passages in our lives, so that an increasing part of our past experience is excluded from most of our personal relations. The inevitable result is that as men grow older they come to feel more solitary, and when they meet a friend of long ago, this feeling is suddenly relieved.

There is, however, another element more profound than this. The flight of time, the transitoriness of all things, the empire of death, are the foundations of tragic feeling. Ever since men began to reflect deeply upon human life, they have sought various ways of escape: in religion, in philosophy, in poetry, in history – all of which attempt to give eternal value to what is transient. While personal memory persists, it, in some degree, postpones the victory of time and gives persistence, at least in recollection, to the momentary event. The same impulse carried further causes kings to engrave their victories on monuments of stone, poets to relate old sorrows in words whose beauty (they hope) will make them immortal, and philosophers to invent systems proving that time is no more than an illusion. Vain effort! The stone crumbles, the poet's words become unintelligible, and the philosopher's systems are forgotten. Nonetheless, striving after eternity has ennobled the passing moment.

4 January 1933

Success and Failure

Free competition, which was the watchword of nineteenth-century liberalism, had undoubtedly much to be said in its favour. It increased the wealth of the nations, and it accelerated the transition from handicrafts to machine industry; it tended to remove artificial injustices and realised Napoleon's ideal of opening careers to talent. It left, however, one great injustice unremedied – the injustice due to unequal talents. In a world of free competition the man whom Nature has made energetic and astute grows rich, while the man whose merits are of a less competitive kind remains poor.

The result is that the gentle and contemplative types remain without power, and that those who acquire power believe that their success is due to their virtues. The underdog remains, therefore, without any champions possessing the kind of ability that leads to success.

In old days this was not the case, and from this point of view certain social advantages accrued through persecution wherever it was not too severe. A man like Cromwell would, in the modern world, have risen to power without being obliged to be a revolutionary; what made him revolutionary was the persecution of his co-religionists. In the days when science was persecuted by the Church, men of science were liberal and progressive; nowadays, when they are covered with honours and universally respected, they tend to be supports of the *status quo*.

The most prominent champions of the wage earners in their struggle for tolerable conditions of life were, at least on the continent of Europe, with few exceptions, Jews. If their Judaism had not made them victims of social injustice, they would not have had so much sympathy with those who suffered from other forms of oppression.

The qualities that make for success in practical life are not always those that have the greatest social utility; many inventors, for example, have died poor, while business men made vast fortunes out of their brains. Apart from such exceptional cases, the ordinary plain citizen, who is easy-going and a trifle stupid, and perhaps not very energetic, deserves consideration, but cannot champion his own cause effectively, because he does not possess the necessary push.

What is the poor fellow to do? He must search for someone of a different type from himself, who will nevertheless look after his interests. The successful politician succeeds in persuading the ordinary citizen that he is such a man, but unless the successful politician has some reason for feeling a grudge against society, such as comes from belonging to a persecuted race or sect, he will, as soon as he is successful, think that all is right with the world and begin to despise the discontents of average men by means of which he has risen to power.

It is hard on a man to be born stupid, and, in a world of free competition, this initial misfortune will be aggravated by the fact that he will achieve no success. The stupid cannot be successfully championed by one of themselves, and there is nothing like a little persecution for making a clever man feel sympathy for those who are not clever. I do not, of course, argue seriously that persecution, however mild, can be defended on this ground; I merely note that the champions it has given to the cause of the oppressed are some slight offset to its other evils.

People destitute of the arts of success have their rights, and it is difficult to say how they are to secure them when all those who possess these arts achieve success. There is no solution except to abandon the belief that competition is a means of securing justice.

11 January 1933

On Feeling Ashamed

Most people, at any rate most young people, know the feeling of a sudden humiliating recollection, when one goes hot all over and stops breathing for a moment. If in company I have told a story which was too long and failed to raise the expected laugh, or which was tactless in view of some person's presence, I am apt to wake up in the middle of the night with a hot feeling of shame, of which the cause for a moment escapes me and then suddenly rushes back into memory. The same sort of thing happens when one has been ignorant of something one ought to have known, and more particularly if one has failed to recognise a person who is hurt at being forgotten. I suspect that Lord Rolle, who rolled down the steps of the throne at Queen Victoria's coronation, could never after hear about rolling without a blush.[22] I still remember with a profound sense of guilt an occasion on which I forgot a dinner engagement and remembered just as I had finished my own dinner. I rushed round, arriving very late, and tried to eat a second dinner, which I found to be an agonising torture. To the young and shy the recollection of social *faux pas* is a misery which makes society much more painful than solitude.

I think the feeling that most people have about serious sins is essentially of the same kind. Those who commit a murder – so, at least, I gather from the books – feel little remorse so long as they are sure that they will not be found out, but begin to wish that they had not done it as soon as discovery becomes imminent. I doubt whether there is any real difference, except in degree, between the remorse of a murderer and the humiliation of the shy man when he has behaved awkwardly. In each case one has the feeling 'If only it were to do again, how differently I could act,' combined with fantasies of a wiser behaviour which may in time completely falsify one's memory. I suspect that nine people out of ten, if they had committed a murder at the age of twenty and had never been found out, would by the time they were seventy have become convinced that they had never done any such thing. I am sure that eminent plutocrats who are self-made have quite forgotten the tricks and twists of their early days. Public exposure of crimes committed long ago, when it occurs, probably causes genuine surprise to the criminal. I read a novel once in which a man and woman, who had both committed serious crimes, married each other in ignorance of each other's past and were both genuinely pained when they discovered the sort of person they had married. I think remorse is essentially a social phenomenon which occurs when we realise that, owing to something we have done, we cannot make other people take that favourable view of ourselves that we should wish them to entertain. It is, of course, essential that we should accept the standards from which our social condemnation springs. If we do not, our reaction is quite different, being one of indignation and self-assertion.

Some fortunate people never experience the sense of being in the wrong, either in great matters or in small. I remember once asking an eminent lady whether she had ever felt shy. She replied: 'No. Whenever I have felt any tendency that way, I have said to myself "You are the cleverest member of one of the cleverest families of the cleverest class of the cleverest nation in the world – why should *you* feel shy?"' I heard this answer with awe and envy.

18 January 1933

On Economic Security

The present age differs from the past in many respects. Perhaps not the least important of these is that, in former times, political power belonged to men who from their infancy had been assured of a comfortable income. In France until the Revolution, and in England until the present century, most aristocrats derived a comfortable income from their estates; they might, it is true, gamble it away, but even then it was generally possible – in France by a position at court, in England by an enclosure act – to retrieve the spendthrift's fallen fortunes. The laws were made by those who had no experience of poverty, no knowledge of the uncertainties of life, no understanding of struggle or competition.

In these opulent societies men had within their own circle a kind of easy good nature which made society very pleasant. They had also the leisure of mind for disinterested curiosity, they travelled in Italy and picked up old masters, they conversed with Arctic explorers and speculated about the Northwest Passage, and they were interested in the experiments of the ingenious Mr Boyle, who was known as the father of chemistry and as the son of the Earl of Cork. In these respects the aristocratic societies which have disappeared were more civilised than the plutocratic societies which have taken their place.

In the world of the present day, a person with a secure income scarcely exists, with the possible exception of those Indian Princes who obtain a salary from the British Government on condition of living in Europe. But even they are likely to lose their means of livelihood if India achieves freedom, since they are not overpopular with their less-fortunate countrymen. Apart from such rare exceptions, those who were rich yesterday are poor today, and those who are rich today know that they are likely to be poor tomorrow. The world is a restless, uneasy, struggling world, in which the leisurely culture of the past is rapidly disappearing.

But when one penetrates ever so little below the surface of the polished societies of the eighteenth century, another side of the picture presents itself. These men, so urbane, so polite, so civilised in their dealings within their own class, were toward other classes ruthless to a degree which democracy has now rendered impossible. The heartlessness of French aristocrats before the Revolution is a commonplace of conventional history, but the English aristocrats of the same period were at least equally ruthless. The French aristocrat was cruel to individuals; the English aristocrat was cruel to whole classes or districts. Between 1760 and 1820, by means of legislation, average wages in England were halved.

Men whose circumstances have always been more comfortable than those of the majority are, as a rule, incapable of sympathy with those who are less fortunate. Sometimes they are frankly callous, sometimes they adopt the more nauseous view that happiness depends upon the soul and is independent of material well-being, so that they are doing no real harm to the poor in taking more than their share of this world's goods. Security depending upon exceptional privilege is unjust, and the man who has to find excuses for an injustice by which he profits is bound to acquire a distorted moral sense. On the other hand, the powerful men of the present day who are the victors in a free fight overestimate the value of ruthlessness and of the various acts by which success in competition is achieved.

There is only one way of preventing these opposite vices. Security would be good if it were not accompanied by injustice; there should, therefore, be security for all and not only for a fortunate few. This is possible, but not while the present competitive system survives.

25 January 1933

On Tact

Education is, to most young people, a painful process, and not its least painful part is instruction in correct social behaviour. I have sometimes passed children playing in the park and heard them say in a loud, clear voice, 'Mummy, who is that funny old man?' To which comes a shocked, subdued, 'Hush! Hush!' The children become dimly aware that they have done something wrong but are completely at a loss to imagine what it is. All children occasionally get presents that they do not like and are instructed by their parents that they must seem to be delighted with them. As they are also informed that they ought not to tell lies, the result is a moral confusion. By the time we grow up we have learned to keep the virtues of tact and truthfulness in watertight compartments and to know which are the occasions for the one and which for the other.

It cannot be denied that tact is a virtue. The sort of person who always manages to blurt out the tactless thing, apparently by accident, is a person full of dislike of his or her fellow creatures. But although tact is a virtue, it is very closely allied to certain vices; the line between tact and hypocrisy is a very narrow one. I think the distinction comes in the motive: when it is kindliness that makes us wish to please, our tact is the right sort; when it is fear of offending, or desire to obtain some advantage by flattery, our tact is apt to be of a less amiable kind. Men accustomed to difficult negotiations learn a kind of tenderness towards the vanity of others and indeed towards all their prejudices, which is infinitely shocking to those who make a cult of sincerity. George Fox, like all early Quakers, objected to conventional forms of respect as savouring of idolatry. When, by order of King Charles II, an officer came to arrest him, the officer, who was a gentleman and did not like the job, took off his hat to Fox, who retorted by exclaiming, 'Repent, thou beast!' It was not the officer's arresting him that he minded, but his taking off his hat.

Men who are profoundly in earnest have always had this dislike of tact. When Beethoven went to visit Goethe at Weimar, he could not bear to see the great man behaving politely at Court to a set of fools. Kropotkin relates how the early Russian revolutionaries, many of whom were aristocratic, deliberately abandoned all forms of politeness. I have known myself men who were in all circumstances sincere and never told a polite lie, and I have found that their genuineness was appreciated and that what in others would have been thought rude gave no offence when coming from them. They have made me feel ashamed of practising politeness, and yet I have never ventured to imitate them.

I think the gist of the matter is that a saint can live without politeness, and indeed that politeness is incompatible with a saintly character. But the man who is always to be sincere must be free from spite and envy and malice and pettiness. Most of us have a dose of these vices in our composition and therefore have to exercise tact to avoid giving offence. We cannot all be saints, and if saintliness is impossible, we may at least try not to be too disagreeable.

1 February 1933

Changing Fashions in Reserve

At all times there have been some things about which it was correct to boast, other things about which men boasted when they were drunk or excited, and yet other things about which they kept silent. But the fashion of these things has changed very notably during my lifetime. The Victorian was proud of his deep feeling and his manly self-control. He wished it to be guessed that his heart was broken without his having to say so in explicit terms, without any hint from him as to the tragic incident by which life had been blighted. There should be as little external action as possible; the drama should be, as far as may be, confined within his own soul. Byron had set the fashion but somewhat crudely. As time went on refinements were introduced but without essential alteration.

Young men and women of the present day are very different – those, at least, who are really up to date. They wish you to think that there is no end to the daring things they have done, but that they have never felt an emotion of any sort while doing them. In actual fact they have often felt far more emotion than was felt by their Byronic grandfathers, but they are ashamed of it. They despise what used to be called sensibility, and the more they have, the less they pretend to have. In old days a poet tried to persuade you how deeply he had loved, while concealing the names of the objects of his passion; the modern poet does not mind the names being known, but would hate it to be supposed that his heart had been involved.

All reserve is based upon fear, and the change in the kind of reserve that is practised is due to the fact that men's fears are different from what they used to be. In old days there was a very rigid code of respectability and manners which a man infringed at his peril, but he was all the more highly thought of if he suffered pain while obeying the code. The modern young man is more afraid of the ridicule of contemporaries if he should for a moment fall into the type of humbug which has made their elders odious to them. Of course avoidance of humbug, when it is once erected into a rigid principle, becomes itself a source of a new kind of humbug. But this kind has not become disgusting to the young, since they have not seen it practised by those who had power over them. Their children, I suppose, will yearn for a little emotionalism in their parents, and will react again towards sensibility. One thing constant throughout the ages is the belief that old people are tiresome and absurd – a most wholesome belief, since it is the cause of progress. The only periods for which there is no hope are the periods in which the young respect the old.

This change in the nature of reserve is one of the chief reasons that have made it difficult for the old to understand the young, and for the young to respect the old. The old appear to the young indecently blatant about their fine feelings, and the young seem to the old indecently blatant about their un-fine doings. In actual fact the old are not such humbugs as they seem to the young, nor are the young as hard-boiled as they seem to the old. The old have their moments of sincerity, and the young have their moments of pretence. But when the young pretend, they pretend to the very opposite of what the old would pretend to, and when the old are sincere, their sincerity is of a sort to which the young are blinded by their code. Misunderstandings between old and young depend not only upon the fact that the old have power, but also upon the changes in the world; as these changes grow more rapid, the misunderstandings are likely to grow greater until all real converse between persons of different generations becomes impossible. This is to be regretted, but can hardly be avoided until the world has become more stable.

8 February 1933

On Honour

In Bernard Shaw's play, *How He Lied to Her Husband*, the lady says to her lover: 'As a gentleman and a man of honour you couldn't tell the truth.'

This illustrates the very peculiar position that honour occupies among moral principles. Many things are wicked but not dishonourable; some things are virtuous but not honourable. Wherever a code of honour exists, it is considered more imperative than the ordinary moral code. Prussian officers in old days used to be exonerated for military disobedience if they had been commanded to do something contrary to their honour. It was compatible with honour to ruin Europe in warfare against Napoleon, but it would have been dishonourable to employ private assassins to remove him without damage to anyone else; in fact, the British Government repeatedly refused with indignation the offers of would-be murderers. A gentleman's honour used to suffer if he endured an insult without allowing the offender a chance to run him through the body with a rapier or shoot him through the head with a pistol. When the Emperor of Russia promised the King of Prussia to make his dominions as large as they had been before Napoleon cut them in two, honour demanded that he should carry out his undertaking even if he had to force unwilling populations to submit to Prussian dominion and to risk a European war in process. The honour of the merchant demands that he shall pay his debts but not that he shall avoid sharp dealing. The honour of a card player demands that he shall make money by only one sort of skill and not by another. The honour of a woman demands only one thing and ignores the whole of the rest of the moral code.

Honour as a guide to behaviour is becoming obsolete. It flourished most in aristocratic societies where everybody knew everybody and the niceties of behaviour were canvassed in gossip. Honourable behaviour, broadly speaking, was such as caused a man to be respected by his equals. If he broke promises to them, he was ill thought of, but he might break promises to his social inferiors as much as he liked. Throughout history it will be found that kings have broken faith with their subjects whenever they dared. The conception of honour is bound up with the idea of life as a courtly game which could not be played with enjoyment unless everybody obeyed its rules. The rules do not serve any purpose outside themselves, any more than do the rules of chess or bridge; they are merely such as are thought likely to give zest to the game. In serious times honour as a rule of conduct tends to disappear. Cromwell, in the creation of his army, made it a principle that to men of honour must be opposed men of religion, and it turned out that religion could inspire quite as much courage on the battlefield as was inspired in the king's army by love of glory.

However curious some forms of honour may be, any recognised code has the advantage that people can count on each other in certain respects. It is very pleasant, for example, to be able to count on one's friends not to repeat secrets that they have been told in confidence. I doubt whether a really agreeable and civilised social life is possible without some code of honour, although many of the codes of honour which have in fact existed were obstacles to pleasant social intercourse. While duelling prevailed, rudeness from one man to another was more tolerated than it is now because the duel wiped out the offence. Although many forms of honour are fantastic, some kind of honour is necessary to a pleasant society. To this extent honour serves a useful purpose, but when treated as the source and fount of all excellence it becomes an obstacle to everything of real importance.

15 February 1933

The Consolations of History

Ever since the time of Boethius in the sixth century it has been customary to speak of the consolations of philosophy, but for my part I find more consolation to be derived from the study of history. When a child is unhappy, his whole horizon is bounded by his misery, and the earlier and later times of his own life become dim. As we grow older we become able to remember when we have the toothache that it will not last for ever. The same kind of comfort which we thus derive from our own past experience can be derived in even greater measure from the past history of mankind. The world is in a bad way at present, and those who know no history are inclined to suppose that it has never been in such a state before. This point of view leads to despair and apathy.

In actual fact, however, the world has often been in a worse state than it is now. The average European, say in the year 1819, was pretty certainly more unhappy than he is now. There was more actual hunger, there was more wickedness in high places, there was more fear of oppression on the one hand and of revolution on the other; young children worked for fifteen hours a day in factories, and the wages of an agricultural labourer were about two dollars a week. Shelley described the politicians of his time as

> . . . Rulers who neither see, nor feel, nor know,
> But leech-like to their fainting country cling,
> Till they drop, blind in blood, without a blow. . . .[23]

We may not have any very high opinion of our present politicians, but most of us would hardly describe them quite so savagely as this. In the same poem he describes George III as 'an old, mad, blind, despised, and dying king'. Shelley's despair was that of all generous minds. The hopes aroused by the French

Revolution were dead, and in a dull peace of exhaustion the reactionary Eastern Powers repressed all attempts at improvement. Nevertheless within thirty years the world had entered upon a period of buoyant optimism and unexampled prosperity.

The chief difficulty for men, as for other animals, is adaptation to new circumstances. The great reptiles of the days before men, who might have seemed invincible, perished from a change of climate. Innumerable kinds of animals have become extinct through specialising on weapons of offence, such as too many horns, which left them inadequate energy for ordinary living. Man, however, has survived the Ice Age, wars, pestilences, and all the other dangers which have threatened his existence. Each change has been met by an adaptation much slower than it need have been, since it was always opposed by what we call practical men, i.e. those who blindly followed the revered wisdom of their ancestors. Such men still control our politics and make our adaptation to the altered circumstances of industrialism much slower than it need be. But in the long run everybody will see that in a rapidly changing world wisdom cannot consist in mere adherence to tradition. As soon as we allow intelligence instead of passion to guide our economic life, we shall all grow rich. Most people find it pleasanter to follow their passions rather than their intelligence, but when the penalty is starvation, they will, in the long run, submit to being reasonable. The conditions of universal prosperity are quite simple and well known, but they involve changes in our habits of feeling, and will, therefore, only be adopted when the lessons of the Depression have sunk deep into men's minds.

22 February 1933

Is Progress Assured?

During the past half-century, knowledge of all kinds has increased with unexampled rapidity, but in few directions has the advance been more striking than in regard to early man. Children beginning the study of history can nowadays be told of the primitive races and of their gradual progress and usually find this much more interesting than the dry records of intertribal warfare in Greece, Italy, or Britain with which the teaching of history formerly began. A little book, *The Long Road from Savagery to Civilisation* by Fay-Cooper Cole (Baltimore: William & Wilkins, 1933), tells the story in a way likely to hold the attention of any intelligent boy or girl. Anthropologists and archaeologists have discovered more than anyone fifty years ago would have supposed possible about the history of man before the invention of writing. Bit by bit, through stone implements, domestication of animals, agriculture, bronze, and iron, man acquired mastery of his environment and rose from being a rare species at the mercy of wild animals to being the lord of creation and the commonest of the larger mammals.

History in this bird's-eye view is encouraging and wholesome. It views mankind as a whole, not through the distorting lenses of national or racial prejudice. It shows progress predominating over retrogression and new arts giving new possibilities of civilised life. This long-range optimism is probably justified and affords a legitimate consolation in a period of depression and difficulty such as that in which we live. The little book to which I alluded ends with the statement: 'We face the future with a confidence born of achievement.' As regards the distant future, such confidence is probably justified.

But as regards the nearer future – say, the next 200 years – no such confidence is warranted by history. If you had lived in the Roman Empire in the year 400 AD and had been gifted with the power of foreseeing the future, you would have known that civilisation, throughout the whole region in which it was most highly developed, was about to suffer eclipse and that during the next two centuries it would suffer a setback from which it would not fully recover for 800 years.

Nor was this a unique occurrence. The Egyptian and Babylonian civilisations were impaired, and the Minoan civilisation was destroyed, by barbarian invaders. The Moslem civilisation, after a brilliant beginning, decayed through internal dissensions. China and Japan have frequently suffered centuries of eclipse through civil war. To this day the Near East is less civilised than it was 2,000 years ago. Civilisations which have not been destroyed by external enemies have frequently suffered from internal decay.

In old days there were many civilisations and many nations still untouched by civilisation. Now, the world is becoming a unity, dominated by the industrial system which, beginning in the north of England about 150 years ago, has already spread to all the great nations and acquired control of all the main economic resources. If it decays, it cannot be regenerated from without; if it destroys itself in internecine wars, there will be no fresh races to build upon the ruins. This is a new fact of our age, which makes inferences from past history somewhat precarious.

For this reason among others, if progress is to continue, it must be more deliberately planned, more based upon social science, than the progress of former ages. We have based our daily life to such an extent upon scientific knowledge and technique that we must go on along the same road: if we leave parts of our social life at the mercy of primitive barbarism, they will destroy the other parts and bring the whole human race to destruction. There is in our time a tendency to exalt the elements of unreason which we have inherited from our barbarous past; but we cannot combine these elements with scientific technique. Those who praise them should give up industrialism, let nine-tenths of our population die of hunger, and revert to bows and arrows. If they will not face this alternative, they must become civilised in their passions, not only in their command over natural forces.

19 February 1934

Right and Might[24]

'Universal sovereignty does not belong to any individual to the exclusion of all the rest, and no one ever saw a dynasty which could count a hundred generations of emperors. Possession – and possession only – gives a right to govern.'

If you have friends interested in history and political theory, you may safely ask them to guess who said this. Was it Cromwell? Was it Robespierre? Was it some extreme follower of Jefferson? Was it Lenin, or perhaps Hitler? These are some of the guesses likely to be made, but they are all completely wide of the mark. The author of this weighty observation on right and might was Tien Te, the leader of the Taiping rebellion in China, and the date is 1850. He was trying to dispossess the Manchu emperors, who were foreign conquerors, and in the meantime he was not above a little brigandage. 'How', he exclaimed, 'have the Manchus, who are foreigners, a right to collect the revenues of eighteen provinces, while we, who are Chinese, are forbidden to take a little money from the public stock?'

This is an awkward argument, not only in China, but in most of the countries of the world. Everywhere, ownership of land is derived from military force. The great land owners of England owe their title sometimes to William the Conqueror's spoliation of the Saxons, sometimes to Henry VIII's seizure of Church property, and in either case to naked force. In America, the land had to be acquired by force from the Indians. The gold and diamond mines of South Africa, which are the basis of many princely fortunes, were similarly taken from the Negroes. Everywhere, the title to land rests, in the last resort, upon the power of the sword.

Why, then, do we all object to brigandage? We cannot object on the ground that the brigand has no *right* to the rich man's property, since the rich man is merely the descendant or legal heir of some earlier brigand. We object because law and order are desirable, and when men have acquired property by force it is usually desirable to confirm their possession by legal enactment. Within a state, it has been found a good plan to forbid all force except that of the government, in order that people may not lose their time, their money, and even their lives, in fighting each other. The 'right' of a man to his property, in short, is merely a matter of social convenience.

As between different nations, however, the maxims of the worthy Tien Te are universally admitted. A victorious nation has, in practice as well as in theory, the right to extort just as much as it possibly can from its vanquished enemy. This right was exercised by Napoleon, by the Germans in 1871, and by the Allies in 1919. In the relations between different states, we still have the condition of universal brigandage that existed between individuals in the days before there were orderly governments. And we still have all the evils that attended that state: the anarchy is international, not national, but is none the better for that.

It is useless to hope for lasting peace in the world until the relations between different national governments are regulated by law, that is to say, by a force stronger than any of the national governments, and able to enforce its decisions, however unpopular they may be with a section of the human race. You may say, if you please, that you prefer war, with all its horrors, to the surrender of one iota of national sovereignty. This is an intelligible position, though, to my mind, a mistaken one. But you cannot say, with any semblance of logic, that you are against war but in favour of the present system, according to which, in a dispute, every government is the ultimate judge in its own case. If war is ever abolished, it will have to be by the establishment of an international government possessed of irresistible armed forces. And if war is not abolished, civilisation cannot survive. This is a painful dilemma for those whose patriotic feelings are stronger than their reasoning powers, but if it is not apprehended intellectually it will be disastrously proved by the march of events.

Prosperity and Public Expenditure[24]

In the present difficult times, two diametrically opposite policies are urged upon governments by different schools of economists. One school, basing itself upon what would be prudent conduct for an individual when his income diminishes, says: diminish expenditure in every possible way, dismiss employees wherever possible, cut down the wages of the rest, and so make ends meet. The other school says: the depression is caused by insufficient expenditure, and can only be cured by spending more, but since, at the moment, private capitalists are not finding it profitable to spend in the form of new investments, the spending must be by public authorities. The first of these theories has been adopted by the British government, the second by that of the United States. I believe that America is right in this matter, although, from a common sense point of view, it might seem obvious that the way to get over being hard up is to save. Why is common sense wrong about public expenditure, when it would be right if only an individual were concerned?

There is, to begin with, one obvious difference between private and public expenditure. What an individual spends is lost to him, but is not lost to the community. When I buy a pair of shoes, I am poorer, but the shoemaker is richer. When the community spends, it spends on the citizens, and therefore the community is not necessarily impoverished. Whether it is enriched or impoverished will depend upon the kind of expenditure, the system of taxation by which the money is raised, and the general economic situation.

When the state spends money which it has raised by taxation, it is taking money out of the pockets of the taxpayers to put it into the pockets of those upon whom it is spending. The expenditure may be really an investment: education, for instance, is an investment in the young, and is universally recognised as part of the duty of the state. In such a case, provided the investment is sound, public expenditure is obviously justified: the community would not be ultimately enriched by ceasing to educate its children, nor yet by neglecting harbours, roads, and public works generally.

But even when there is no such obvious justification, public expenditure may still, on the balance, be profitable to the community. At a time of wide-spread unemployment, it may be greatly diminished, with the result that many men receive wages who would otherwise be destitute. These men spend their wages, and thereby increase the demand for all that they buy, which helps to restore prosperity to producers of the necessaries of life; these producers in turn spend their increased profits, probably in part in increased wages, since they are likely to employ more men. To this process it is hard to set a limit, and thus prosperity may spread to ever-widening circles.

Meanwhile, of course, if the public expenditure is financed by taxes, the taxpayers have less to spend. If it is financed by loans, those who lend cannot invest the money elsewhere. Does this loss counterbalance the gain? In good times, perhaps it does, since the money lent to the state would otherwise have been invested in industry. But in bad times, such as the present, much of the money would have lain idle; to that extent, therefore its employment in public expenditure is an uncompensated gain.

It seems to follow that, in times like the present, when there are very many unemployed, and private capital is afraid of new enterprises, public expenditure is almost certain to prove beneficial, provided it is wisely directed. This is the more true because an atmosphere of hopefulness can be created. Depressions, as everyone recognises, are largely psychological; therefore some real benefit is likely to result from whatever is widely believed to be beneficial.

Public and Private Interests [24]

In the days when political economy was still young and aggressive, economists taught that there is an essential harmony between public and private interests. 'Consider Mr Zedekiah Stubbins,' they would say. 'He has, as you know, acquired a considerable fortune by cotton spinning' (it was always cotton-spinning in those days) 'and in so doing has been actuated, doubtless, by purely self-regarding motives. But his fortune was due to the cheapness of his product, which benefited all the multitudinous consumers throughout the world. And by the wages paid in his factory he saved from starvation large numbers of men, women, and children, some of the latter still of tender age. Nor did the beneficent effect of his activities cease there; by increasing the demand for cotton goods through greater cheapness, he enriched the cotton planter, and enabled him to be more munificent towards the coloured population dependent on his bounty. All these admirable results have flowed from Mr Stubbins minding his own business.'

Economists were driven to abandon this high ground by the indignation of the general public. It became known that Mr Stubbins made little children work fifteen hours a day, that they had to be beaten with iron rods to keep them awake at their work, and that nevertheless they sometimes fell asleep and were mangled by rolling into the machinery. And slavery on the cotton plantations was, in its way, as bad as wage-slavery in the factories. The law interfered, and Mr Stubbins was forced to be a little less theoretical in his philanthropy.

Nevertheless, the old theory of the harmony between public and private interests lingers on, and is appealed to by the industrial magnates whenever there is any suggestion that their predatory activities might, with advantage, be curtailed. On the other hand, it must be confessed that those who do not think their activities wholly beneficent are too apt to think them wholly harmful, which is just as great an error.

If Mr Stubbins (to return to him) had made his fortune by improved machinery, by better organisation of the processes of production, by more thorough technical training of his more highly paid employees, he would have deserved what the economists said of him. But if he made his fortune by long hours and low wages, by torturing children, by protective tariffs which raised the price of his product and which he secured by political corruption, by robbing inventors of their patents, by lying advertisements, or by any of a hundred and one other tricks of the trade, then, and to that extent, he was not a public benefactor, and his private interest was in conflict with the interest of the general public. If private enterprise is to continue, it is essential that the law should, as far as possible, compel it to confine itself to those methods of making a profit which are advantageous to the public.

In these days, however, this is difficult. The power of the great magnates, through political corruption, through threats of causing a panic, through influence on large sections of the press, is such that, while they may be defeated in a pitched battle at a time of political excitement, they cannot be kept in their place at ordinary times unless, as a result of a pitched battle, they have been shorn of most of their means of influencing opinion. Whether this is possible while they retain their property is a difficult question, as to which we shall know more when the present American experiment has run its course. It may be found necessary to go further than is at present contemplated, but as to that I should not venture on a prophecy.

Notes

1. At the time he wrote this article, Russell himself was fifty-nine. He is referring to the Labour Government of 1929–31, more than half of whose ministers were over sixty, although only four were over seventy.
2. Because of his criticisms of Britain's war-time policies, Russell was imprisoned for four and a half months in 1918. See his *Autobiography*, Vol. II, Chapter 1.
3. Some of the people imprisoned with Russell were conscientious objectors.
4. I.e., shoplifting.
5. See Wayne Andrews, *The Vanderbilt Legend* (New York: Harcourt, Brace, 1941), p. 11. Also Arthur D. H. Smith, *Commodore Vanderbilt* (New York: McBride, 1927), p. 18.
6. *Random Reminiscences of Men and Events* (New York: Doubleday, Page and Co., 1909), p. 33.
7. In his *Areopagitica*.
8. William O. Stapledon, *Last and First Men* (New York: Cape and Smith, 1931; London: Methuen, 1932).
9. Grand Rapids, Michigan, has, from the end of the nineteenth century, been the 'furniture capital of America', i.e. the main centre for mass produced furniture.
10. *An Enquiry Concerning Political Justice* (1793), Vol. II, Book VIII, Chapter VI.
11. This essay is reprinted from *Time and Tide*, 11 June 1932.
12. This essay was first published in *Nash's Pall Mall Magazine*, June 1932.
13. J. L. L. Hammond and B. Hammond, *The Skilled Labourer, 1760–1832* (London: Longmans, Green, 1919; New York: Kelley, 1967), p. 225.
14. The conference Russell means met in February 1932 under the auspices of the League of Nations. It achieved virtually nothing because of the irreconcilable and inflexible demands of the participants.
15. The British Prime Minister at the time this essay appeared was J. Ramsay MacDonald. He had resigned from his position of leadership of the Labour Party in 1914 in protest at its approval of British participation in the First World War.
16. Nathaniel Hawthorne (1850).
17. A commission appointed by President Herbert Hoover and headed by George W. Wickersham which reported in 1931 on the status of the observance and enforcement of federal law.
18. Revd W. L. Tudor, in *The Times* (London), 9 August 1932, p. 6.

19 In 1913, 2,079 children in Great Britain were sentenced to be whipped. In 1927, the number had dropped to 230; in 1930, to 100. See *The Times* (London), 10 June 1932, p. 7. In May 1932 the House of Commons voted to abolish whipping of children. The House of Lords voted on 9 June to restore it; on 30 June the House of Commons unanimously confirmed its earlier action; on 7 July the Lords again vetoed its abolition. It was not until 1948 that the power of the courts to prescribe flogging was drastically reduced. It is still possible in cases of mutiny, incitement to mutiny, and attack on prison officers.

20 C. C. F. Greville, *The Greville Memoirs; a Journal of the Reigns of King George IV and King William IV* (London: Longmans, Green, 1875), Vol. II, p. 229.

21 Greville, *The Greville Memoirs; a Journal of the Reign of Queen Victoria* (London: Longmans, Green, 1885), Vol. I, p. 44.

22 Ibid., pp. 107–8.

23 From 'Sonnet, England in 1819'.

24 This essay has not previously been published.

RUSSELL AT ROUTLEDGE